TESHUVAH ECLIPSES

RON ALLEN

CREATION
HOUSE

Teshuvah Eclipses: The Invitation and the Warning
by Ron Allen
Published by Creation House
A Charisma Media Company
600 Rinehart Road
Lake Mary, Florida 32746
www.charismamedia.com

Cover design by Judith McKittrick Wright

Visit the author's website: www.starbiblesociety.com

Library of Congress Cataloging-in-Publication Data: 2017940075
International Standard Book Number: 978-1-62999-223-5
E-book International Standard Book Number: 978-1-62999-224-2

First edition

17 18 19 20 21 — 987654321

Printed in the United States of America

TABLE OF CONTENTS

PREFACE

O N AUGUST 21, 2017, a sign from God is going to appear in the heavens at midday and streak across America. The sign, a solar eclipse, will appear on the first day of the forty-day Jewish season of Teshuvah, a season of repentance and return to God leading up to the Day of Atonement.

Solar eclipses are very different from lunar eclipses, which have been popularized in recent years. In a lunar eclipse, the moon moves slowly into Earth's shadow. As the eclipse approaches totality, the sun's rays are refracted through Earth's atmosphere, and the moon turns the reddish color that gives lunar eclipses the name *blood moons*. Lunar eclipses occur at night and are normally visible from about half of Earth's surface.

As we have learned in recent years, blood moons play an important role in God's revelation.[1] On the Hebrew lunar calendar, the only calendar God uses, blood moons can occur on the feast days of Passover or Tabernacles. These feast days prophetically point to the shedding of Christ's blood as our Passover sacrifice and the ingathering of God's family at the Feast of Tabernacles. The blood moons are a sign of the Holy Spirit's outpouring and salvation (Acts 2:17–21) and the overcoming of evil by the blood of the Lamb and the Word of our testimony (Rev. 12:11).

On the other hand, solar eclipses occur when the moon comes between the sun and Earth and the shadow of the moon moves across Earth's surface. Unlike the lunar eclipse, which can normally be seen from half of Earth, a total solar eclipse can only be seen in a strip of land about sixty miles wide. The total solar eclipse will travel thousands of miles but will only be visible for about two minutes in any location. Only a small area of land is covered by a solar eclipse.

The early stages of a solar eclipse are barely noticeable. As the moon covers the sun, there is not a visible decrease in the sun's brightness. The outline of the moon can be only seen through thick lenses, like welder's glass[2] (looking directly into the sun will blind a person), or in the shadows under a leafy tree. Then, as totality approaches, the atmosphere changes. A chill breeze blown in from the path of totality arrives. This can be startling and even frightening to the uninitiated. It is a reminder of the darkness of the Day of the Lord (Amos 5:20) and the judgment of God. On the Hebrew feast calendar, the only one that occurs on the first day of the lunar month when solar eclipses can occur is the Feast of Trumpets, which celebrates the second coming of Jesus on the Day of the Lord. Thus, the solar eclipse is a warning of judgment to come.

Once the shock of the arrival of totality passes, a great, glorious picture appears in the sky. The sun and moon come together, symbolizing the unity of the believers, who are represented by the moon (Ps. 89:37), in the sun, which represents Christ (Ps. 19:4–5). Surrounding the united sun and moon is the corona, or crown, of the sun, which is only visible during an eclipse. There is no better sign of unity of Christ and His church, symbolizing the prayer of Christ in John 17.

Teshuvah, the forty-day season of repentance, begins on the first day of the sixth month known an Elul, and the solar eclipses that occur on Teshuvah add to the meaning of Teshuvah. The Teshuvah eclipses are signs of coming judgment, like the Trumpets eclipses, but they are also signs of unity in the presence of God. Thus, the Teshuvah eclipses are both an invitation to return to God and a warning of judgment.

During the eclipse, the moon represents the believers and unites with the sun, which represents Christ. God's Teshuvah eclipse invitation has been accepted by many great church leaders in the last five hundred years, including Martin

Luther, Saint Francis Xavier, Count Nicolaus Zinzendorf, George Whitfield, William Carey, Dr. David Livingstone, Hudson Taylor, William J. Seymour, and Billy Graham. Some of the greatest revivals, including the first and second Great Awakenings, the Azusa Street Revival, the Charismatic Renewal, and the rise of messianic Judaism, have been birthed or nurtured during Teshuvah eclipse years.

Teshuvah eclipses have marked the rise of the United States and Israel as nations. The Teshuvah eclipses have also given prophetic warnings for nations to repent or face disasters. Some of the more significant disasters include the French Revolution, the American Civil War, World War I, the Russian Revolution, the Holocaust, World War II, and the September 11, 2001, terror attack on the United States.

Teshuvah eclipses are the inflection points of destiny, when mankind chose to follow God or not, to obey Him or not, and to live or die.

On Teshuvah 2017 God is inviting His people to unite with Him, resisting temptation as Jesus did in His forty-day Teshuvah fast. We are invited to make the Teshuvah journey of repentance and uniting with Christ.

God is inviting His church to repent and unite in Him as well. As we unite with Christ, we will also find that we are all united in Christ, together as Christians, healing divisions and preparing the way for a great revival.

But the path of the eclipse over the United States is also a solemn warning to return as a nation to our Christian foundation. We ignored God's warning in the Teshuvah eclipse years of 1998 and 1999 and suffered from the terrorist attack of September 11, 2001. We ignored the warning of the 2008 Teshuvah eclipse year and suffered economic disaster and national decline. God has given us another opportunity to heal our land in 2017, and we can repent and return to

Him if the church will unite and make its Teshuvah journey of repentance.

We at the International Star Bible Society urge you to accept the Teshuvah invitation to repent, return to God, and unite in Christ. We also invite you to make a Teshuvah pilgrimage to experience the Teshuvah eclipse and join us in forty days of Teshuvah prayer.

Let us pray that the church and the nation will heed the Teshuvah warning to heal our land before it is too late.

> *Those who cannot remember the past are condemned to repeat it.*
>
> —GEORGE SANTAYANA[3]

PART I

THE APPOINTED TIME OF TESHUVAH

The heavens declare the glory of God.

—Psalm 19:1

In the heavens he has pitched a tent for the sun, which is like a bridegroom coming forth from his pavilion, like a champion rejoicing to run his course.

—Psalm 19:4–5

CHAPTER 1

DISCOVERING THE TESHUVAH ECLIPSES

O<small>N</small> S<small>EPTEMBER</small> 11, 2001, the world watched in horror as the World Trade Center towers burned and then collapsed. We Christians wondered how God could let such a thing happen.

Many years later, it is apparent that God sent a prophet and a sign in the heavens to invite us to repent and save ourselves from disaster. We did not heed God's warning, and we suffered the consequences.

In 2017 God is sending us another sign in the heavens, a solar eclipse at the beginning of the Hebrew season of Teshuvah. Once again, God will invite us to repent and return to Him and warn us of dangers to come if we do not. Once again, we will have to make the choice of whether to follow God and receive blessings or not to and be cursed.

Our path to discovery of this sign in the heavens began in the summer of 1998. It was then that our prayer group, inspired by a prophecy that Chuck Pierce released to the body of Christ, decided to pray and seek the Lord during the Hebrew season of Teshuvah.

Teshuvah is a compound word consisting of the Hebrew *Tashan*, meaning "return," and *hey*, the last letter of the *Jhvh* name for God. The *hey* in *Jhvh* represents the Shekinah, or manifest presence of God. Thus, Teshuvah is a time to return to the presence of God. It is also understood that returning to God is accompanied by repentance.

Teshuvah occurs during the forty days between the first day of the sixth month of the Jewish religious calendar and the Day of Atonement, on the tenth day of the seventh month. Observant Jews have an understanding that this forty-day period, and

especially the last ten days between the Feast of Trumpets and
the Day of Atonement, represents an opportunity to repent and
avoid the judgment of God. For Christians, these forty days are
an invitation to repent and enter into unity with God through
the blood of Christ. However, for unbelievers, Teshuvah is a
solemn warning of the judgment to come.

This duality of Teshuvah—as an invitation and a warning—
is illustrated in two of the scriptures that are associated with
it. Psalm 27 speaks to the benefits of living in God's presence
and seeking His face. He will keep us in time of trouble and
allow us to see His goodness while we live. In Ezekiel 33 the
Lord commands us to warn the unbelievers to repent and save
themselves from the judgment to come. We are also told that
we must warn the righteous of their folly so they can repent,
lest they suffer judgment. Thus, Teshuvah calls believers to
repent and come into God's presence and also calls on us to
evangelize a lost and dying world.

TESHUVAH 1998: DALLAS

On July 8, 1998, prophet Chuck Pierce gave a prophetic word
of invitation and warning that identified a forty-day period
of cleansing from defilement and idolatry between July and
October.[1] This period was clearly recognizable as the forty-day
Teshuvah season, which ran from August 22, 1998, to
September 30, 1998. Our prayer group started praying during
Teshuvah as the word from God had instructed, but it was not
until later that we really understood the message we had been
given.

In the prophecy God identified three major issues that
would challenge the church. First, the church had become
brittle and inflexible and would have to change its governmental
administration. The second challenge was the rapid rise of
Islamic government around the world and even in the United
States. Lastly, there was a spirit of lawlessness that was rising
rapidly and would be attached to the United States and its
government.

God invited the church to repent of its defilement and idolatry during Teshuvah and to receive His plans concerning the next three years. If the church prayed and followed God's plans, a new structure would arise that would be more flexible and able to survive the shaking to come. There would be blessings and favor as the church shook off discouragement, disillusion, and disinterest. God would visit New York, Washington, DC, Detroit, Miami, Houston, Dallas, and Phoenix and would also move in Rome and Greece. The new church structure God wanted to bring into being would have the power to overcome the challenges of Islamic government and lawlessness.

God also warned us of what would happen if we did not repent. If the church did not follow God's plan for building over the next three years, the plan the church followed would not come from Him and would fail. Failure to repent would also not stop the disaster that was set to occur in the United States. The nation would be in crisis and chaos by 2004 if we did not seek God.

As we began praying, we paid no attention to the solar eclipse of August 22, which occurred on the first day of Teshuvah. We did not understand the seriousness of the prophecy spoken by Chuck Pierce or the sign of the Teshuvah eclipses until much later.

TESHUVAH 1999: FRANCE

In the summer of 1999, our group of intercessors made a prayer journey to France to intercede for the church and the nation of France.

Our prayer assignment took us to many places in France, from the ancient Celtic site and cathedral of Chartres to modern Parisian strongholds of secularism, such as *La Madeleine*, a church which memorializes the pantheon of the godless French Revolution. We scheduled our visit to Reims, the coronation city of French kings, to coincide with a solar eclipse that would be visible there on August 11, 1999. It seemed like all of Europe was in Reims for the eclipse, and the weather was cloudy. But, the clouds opened, and we were able to pray through the eclipse.

After the two minutes of totality in Reims in 1999, the path of totality sped off across Europe, through Iran and Afghanistan, and then on through Asia.[2] We prayed there would be repentance in the French church and an outpouring of the Spirit. We did not connect the 1999 Teshuvah eclipse to the prophetic word given by Chuck Pierce in 1998 until much later. As the Teshuvah eclipses of 1998 and 1999 passed into history, the prophecy of Chuck Pierce faded from memory as well. However, the Word of God does not return void, and from this distance, it is clear to see the church was being warned of major, historic threats. It is also clear that the church did not accept God's invitation to repent and avert disaster.

Things started happening during Teshuvah of 1998. On September 11, 1998, it was publicly revealed that Bill Clinton, the president of the United States, had committed adultery, abused an intern, abused his power, and then lied to the American people—and while under oath. When President Richard Nixon had been caught lying in 1974, members of the political party that voted him into office went to the White House to force Nixon's resignation. In 1998, members of the political party that voted Bill Clinton into office went to the White House and announced that they would keep him in office despite his immorality and lawbreaking.

As a result, a spirit of lawlessness was loosed on the nation, as warned by Chuck Pierce. President Clinton was impeached but, as promised, his supporters kept him in office. The subsequent election of 2000 left much bitterness, as the political party that had supported him lost in a controversial election. The bitterness led to destructive partisanship and a lawless disregard for the good of the nation. One of the most damaging instances of this lawless behavior was the sabotage by Clinton's party of the oversight of government mortgage companies, which led to the financial collapse of 2008.[3] The new Obama administration, elected in 2008, escalated partisan bitterness and established a policy of lawlessness, ignoring existing laws and the constitutional checks and balances. During this administration, lawlessness produced the forced acceptance of gay marriage, increased crime from political abuse of police, and attacks on freedom of religion.

Obviously, the church had failed to repent and follow the three-year plan outlined in the Pierce prophecy. Exactly three years from the announcement of Clinton's immorality, instead of God's plan being in place, almost three thousand Americans died in the September 11, 2001, terrorist attack; almost six thousand were injured. The source of this attack was terrorists living in Afghanistan, one of the countries passed over by the 1999 Teshuvah eclipse. By 2004, the United States toiled in political crisis and in war with the Islamist factions in Afghanistan and Iraq, just as the Pierce prophecy forewarned. Sadly, the Obama administration sacrificed the American victories in Iraq and opened the way for expansion by the Islamists. Today, Islamists threaten the stability of the entire Muslim world, from Morocco to Indonesia. Some European nations who were also in the warning path of the 1999 Teshuvah eclipse have all but been invaded by Islamic terrorists and refugees.

The cities mentioned in Pierce's prophecy have been visited by God either for blessing or judgment based on their response to God's Teshuvah invitation. Prior to the 9/11 attacks on New York, the city had effectively demonstrated to God that He wasn't wanted. President Clinton's abuses and immortality were ignored, and Hillary Clinton, the former first lady, was elected to the US Senate in New York State. The City of New York had no spiritual protection when the attack came. Washington, DC, was also targeted on 9/11, but the attackers failed to strike the main objective, the White House, because President Bush was covered by intercessory prayer. The city of Detroit refused to change its ways and eventually went bankrupt. The cities of

Houston and Dallas became revival centers and have prospered. Rome has seen movement toward unity and revival, while Greece has spent itself into poverty.

The failure of the church to deal with increasing lawlessness and the rise of Islam was caused not only by failure to repent but also by the failure of the church's governmental political strategy. Beginning with Ronald Reagan, much of the evangelical church in the United States had come to believe that political involvement was the way to counteract the increasing secularization and degeneration of American society. The strategy seemed to have worked during the Reagan and first Bush administrations, and it was hoped that the success would be repeated during the second Bush administration. Unfortunately, the United States's population continued to backslide, and the political position of the church has deteriorated to the point that the very right to religious freedom is at risk.

As the church political structure has been shaken, God is taking the church back to its mission of evangelism, for only changed hearts can save a nation. He has made a distinction between those places which follow him, like Dallas and Houston, and these who did not, like New York.

God sent the blood moons of 2014–2015 as a sign that He is pouring out His Spirit to revive us again. Beginning in 2014, an outreach by Pope Francis to Kenneth Copeland, a leader in the charismatic movement, has led to a unity revival in answer to Jesus' prayer in John 17. And, as the church comes together, an evangelical outpouring can come as unity in the church shows the world that God sent Christ to save them.

God is ever faithful, and He is sending new Teshuvah eclipses in 2017 and 2018 to give us another invitation to return to Him and warn the unbelievers.

We must understand how God has set the sign and appointed times of the Teshuvah eclipses so we will not miss out on God's plan for 2017 and 2018.

Chapter 2

THE SIGN OF THE TESHUVAH ECLIPSES

Our journey to understand Teshuvah eclipses begins on the Day of Pentecost, when the apostle Peter referred to the prophecy of Joel as he explained the outpouring of the Holy Spirit:

> *In the last days, God says, I will pour out my Spirit on all people. Your sons and daughters will prophesy, your young men will see visions, your old men will dream dreams. Even on my servants, both men and women, I will pour out my Spirit in those days, and they will prophesy. I will show wonders in the heaven above and signs on the earth below, blood and fire and billows of smoke. The sun will be turned into darkness and the moon to blood before the coming of the great and glorious day of the Lord. And everyone who calls on the name of the Lord will be saved.*
>
> —Acts 2:17–21

Peter is telling us that there is a prophetic link between the Holy Spirit's outpouring, with its attendant prophecies, dreams, and visions, and the signs in the heavens of the dark sun and the blood moon. The dark sun, a solar eclipse, and the blood moon, a lunar eclipse, are prophetic signs given during the church age, before the return of Christ, when salvation is available to all who call on the name of the Lord. Just as the blood moon lunar eclipses on Passover remind us of the blood of Jesus spilled on Passover, the solar eclipses that occur on Teshuvah are prophetic signs reminding us of the Teshuvah season of repentance and to return to God.

Teshuvah eclipses are also part of a celestial revelation of God described in the Bible in Psalm 19:1: "The heavens declare the glory of God." Not only that, but the heavens "pour forth speech" and "reveal knowledge" (v. 2). Further, the apostle Paul states that Psalm 19 reveals the message of Christ (Rom. 10:17–18). This revelation of Christ begins with the symbolism of the sun as a "bridegroom coming out of his chamber" or a "champion rejoicing to run His course" (Ps. 19:5). The story of Christ in the heavens is told as the sun moves through its path in the stars and constellations, known as the zodiac. Other clues coming from Scriptures show that God named the stars (Ps. 147:4; Isa. 40:26) and gathered them into constellations (Job 38:22). By understanding the meanings of the star names and constellations, the story of Christ in the heavens is told.[1]

During the nineteenth century, scholars traced the names of the stars and constellations back to the first human civilizations in Mesopotamia in the Tigris–Euphrates river system area. However, its origins go back to our first parents in the Garden of Eden, who were told by God that a Deliverer, the Seed of the Woman, Christ, would "crush" the head of the serpent, Satan, and be bruised in the heel, the Cross (Gen. 3:15). The constellations of the zodiac, also known as signs, tell the story as follows:

1. Virgo, the virgin: the promised Seed of Woman

2. Libra, the scales: anticipating the Christ

3. Scorpio, the scorpion: the rebellion

4. Sagittarius, the archer: the coming of the Seed of woman

5. Capricorn, the goat: sacrifice and resurrection of the Christ

6. Aquarius, the water pourer: the outpouring of the Holy Spirit

7. Pisces, the fish: the church age

8. Aries, the ram: promised victory of the Lamb of God

9. Taurus, the bull: the return of Christ

10. Gemini, the united: Christ rules on Earth

11. Cancer, the holding place: home of God's people

12. Leo, the lion: Christ rules over all

In addition to the twelve signs, each sign has three constellations associated with it that map out the entire sky into forty-eight constellations, adding more detail to the story. For example, the church is represented by the constellation we call the Big Dipper, known to the Hebrews as the Assembly, the word used in the Greek Bible for the church.

Against the background of the stars are the seven moving bodies, visible to the naked eye, whose symbolism and motions also form a part of the message of the heavens.

1. Sun: Christ, the Light of the world

2. Moon: the bride of Christ, the church

3. Mars: the blood of Christ

4. Mercury: the morning star laid low, Lucifer

5. Jupiter: the suffering Savior

6. Venus: the bright morning star, the Seed of woman, Christ

7. Saturn: the ruler

Thus, the signs in the sun, moon, and stars include the fixed stars and constellations, the sun and moon, the planets, and other unpredictable signs, such as the star of Bethlehem. The

totality of the signs in the heavens form what is called the Star
Bible. It is the Star Bible that pours forth the knowledge of
Christ and sends daily messages from heaven, and there will
be signs in the sun, moon, and stars that accompany the return
of Christ. (See Luke 21:25.)

The Bible also says that God made the sun, moon, and stars
to serve as "signs to mark sacred times, and days and years"
(Gen. 1:14). God established His sacred seasons within the
lunar Hebrew calendar. The first month of the religious year
is in the spring, with the Feast of Passover coming on the
fourteenth day, when the moon is full and lunar eclipses can
occur. The three Feasts of Spring represent the death, burial,
and resurrection of Christ. The fiftieth day after the Sabbath
of Passover week comes Pentecost, representing the coming
of the Holy Spirit and the birth of the church. Then in the
fall, on the first day of the seventh month, comes the Feast of
Trumpets and the new moon, when solar eclipses can occur,
and which is believed to prefigure the second coming of Christ.
The Day of Atonement on the tenth day represents judgment,
and the Feast of Tabernacles, beginning the fifteenth day, looks
forward to ingathering of the church for eternity with God.
As explained previously, the Teshuvah season is a forty-day
time of repentance beginning with the first day of the sixth
month, when there is a new moon and a solar eclipse can occur,
leading up to the judgment of the Day of Atonement.

In the last five hundred years, about thirteen Teshuvah
eclipses have occurred per century. Like the 1998–1999
Teshuvah eclipses, most come as doubles in sequential year
periods, while there are also triad and solo eclipses. Putting
these related groupings of three, two, or one eclipses together
yields about eight sacred Teshuvah seasons per century. Of
these, about three per century contain eclipses where the path
of totality moves through places which are the subject of a

local message, like the 1999 Teshuvah eclipses, which moved over Europe, Iran, and Afghanistan.

Another interesting aspect of the Teshuvah eclipses is their relationship to blood moons. Most of the Teshuvah eclipses are preceded for one or two years by blood moons on Passover and Tabernacles. Specifically, about six Teshuvah eclipse groups per century are preceded by blood moons on Passover and Tabernacles. All four of the modern blood moons tetrads of 1493–1494, 1949–1950, 1967–1968, and 2014–2015 preceded Teshuvah eclipses.

The place to begin to finally understand the role of the Teshuvah eclipses in the Star Bible is with the blood moons. As stated previously, a blood moon is caused when the moon moves into the shadow of the Earth, and the sun's rays are filtered through Earth's atmosphere to produce a reddish color on the moon. In the Star Bible, the sun symbolizes Jesus as a Champion and a Bridegroom (Ps. 19:4–5). The moon represents the believers and the bride of Christ as the "faithful witness in the sky" (Ps. 89:37). The blood moon signifies salvation through the covering of the believers by the blood of Christ. In Acts 2:17–21 Peter, quoting from Joel 2:28–31, associates blood moons with the outpouring of the Spirit and salvation during the church age. Blood moons, the covering of the faithful by the blood of the Lamb, are also symbolic of overcoming evil in Revelation 12:11.[2]

Only fifteen blood moon tetrads have covered the Feasts of Passover and Tabernacles since the original Passover and Exodus thirty-five centuries ago. Nine of these have occurred in the church age, and four have occurred since 1493. The rarity of these events indicates their importance, and our study of the blood moon tetrads shows that each tetrad during the church age has been accomplished by a major expansion of the church. For example, the 1967–1968 blood moon tetrad saw the beginning of the charismatic movement, which has resulted in six hundred million charismatic Christians.

All four of the blood moon tetrads—1493–1494, 1949–1950, 1967–1968, and 2014–2015—are followed after two years by a Teshuvah eclipse grouping. However, many duplex blood moons on Passover and Tabernacles occurred during the last five hundred years, which are also followed after a year or two by a Teshuvah grouping. Those blood moons would also signify the outpouring of the Holy Spirit, salvation, and overcoming evil in the same manner as the tetrads. However, because of their frequency, about five per century, these blood moons would indicate events of lesser impact and a shorter time frame than the blood moon tetrads. Even so, the blood moon duplexes are an important prophetic sign of God's desire to move through His people during Teshuvah.

Teshuvah eclipses, like lunar eclipses, feature the same symbolism of the sun representing Christ and the moon representing believers. However, in a solar eclipse the sun and moon come together in the sky. Here the moon, representing the believers, moves into the sun, representing Christ. To the unbeliever, however, the picture presented by the darkness of the solar eclipse is one of darkness matching the biblical description of the second coming of Christ on the Day of the Lord (Amos 5:20). Thus, the solar eclipse is both a prophetic invitation to be united with Christ in God's presence and a warning of judgment to come.

The Teshuvah season on the Jewish calendar amplifies the invitation and warning because the forty-day period ends on the Day of Atonement, which pictures God's judgment. The position of the sun relative to the Star Bible signs of the zodiac is also significant. Those Teshuvah eclipses, which occur from about August 2 to August 10 in our time, occur while the sun is in Cancer, the sign of the home of God's people and a picture of unity with God. However, Teshuvah eclipses, which occur from about August 11 to September 1, occur in Leo, the sign of God's judgment.

Putting it all together, the blood moon symbolism of salvation and the outpouring of the Spirit; the eclipse symbol of unity in Christ; the Teshuvah period of repentance and returning to God; and the sun in Cancer, the sign of heaven, all point to the Teshuvah eclipses as a prophetic invitation to unite with God in His presence.

On the other hand, the blood moon symbolism of overcoming evil; the eclipse symbol of judgment; the judgment at the end of the Teshuvah period; and the sun in Leo, the sign of judgment, all point to the Teshuvah eclipses as a prophetic warning of judgment to come.

The story of humanity, and the story of the last five hundred years, is the story of how people have chosen to respond to God's invitation to unity and His warning of judgment. As with the 1998–1999 Teshuvah sacred time, the invitation and the warning mark a critical time of decision and the beginning of a process that can play out over decades as the consequences of those decisions manifest themselves.

Teshuvah eclipses are the prophetic inflection points of history, where God gives people the chance to serve Him or not and choose life over death.

TESHUVAH CHOICES

The sun will be turned to darkness and the moon to blood before the coming of the great and glorious day of the Lord. And everyone who calls on the name of the Lord will be saved.

—ACTS 2:20–21

CHAPTER 3

THE BROKEN BODY OF CHRIST

THE YEAR 2017 is a year of anniversaries. First, it marks the five hundredth anniversary of the Protestant Reformation. It is also the fiftieth anniversary of the blood moon tetrad of 1967–1968, which gave rise to the charismatic movement. Finally, it is the fortieth anniversary of the interdenominational charismatic meeting for unity in Kansas City in 1977, where the people prayed for healing for the broken body of Christ.[1]

The Protestant Reformation was not the first division in the body of Christ, and it certainly was not last. Like many church schisms, sincere Christians and martyrs have been on both sides of the divide. It was a tragedy that rocked Europe for two hundred years, leaving scars that are just now being healed. It all began with a sincere man seeking to find acceptance from God in a Teshuvah-like journey of repentance. His name was Martin Luther.

TESHUVAH 1505: GERMANY

God announced Himself to the apostle Paul with a bright light. In the Teshuvah year of 1505, a lightning bolt struck Martin Luther. After he survived the lightning strike, Luther made a vow to serve God and adopted the strict lifestyle of an Augustine monk. But no matter how much self-discipline he endured, he could not escape his sense of condemnation and sinfulness.

Like many sincere Christians, he wanted to take the Teshuvah path of repentance and return to God. He simply did not know how to do it. What Luther learned, as he completed his Teshuvah pilgrimage and found peace with God, changed the world.

Teshuvah 1514: Germany

Luther received his doctorate in theology in the blood moon year of 1512. As Luther looked harder for a way to make the Teshuvah journey, he found himself studying the Scriptures for an answer. In 1515, he found his peace with God when he discovered the words of Romans 1:17, "The just shall live by faith" (nkjv). It was God's grace and mercy that allowed him to return to God through faith in the Cross, the Crucifixion. His insistence that faith alone, not good works, was the key to salvation brought him into conflict with the church doctrine of his day.

As with the 1998 Teshuvah prophecy, his faith was tested years later when the church began selling indulgences, or cash sales of alleged spiritual benefits, to fund St. Peter's Cathedral. On October 31, 1517, Luther nailed his famous Ninety-Five Theses to the door of the Wittenberg Castle Church in his hometown of Wittenberg, Germany. He hoped to bring reform to the church and never imagined what would follow.

Church leaders had their chance to take the Teshuvah path of repentance and return to God. Instead, they chose to persecute Martin Luther. He was only saved from death by Frederick the Wise, who "kidnapped" Luther and took him to a safe place, the Wartburg Castle.

It was not until 1999 that Lutherans and Catholics agreed with Martin Luther that we are saved by grace alone.[2]

Teshuvah 1523 and 1524: Germany

During the blood moon year of 1522, Luther translated the New Testament into German. However, in 1522, he felt compelled to return to Wittenberg to lead the churches that had broken away from the Catholic Church. The newly formed Lutheran churches had their own Teshuvah warnings in 1523 and 1524 as Luther started to establish a new Protestant Church authority. But, many Germans rejected the attempt to maintain order. Their response was to start a rebellion against all authority. Military force crushed the spirit of lawlessness in Germany, but it broke out three years later when an army led by Catholic king Charles V mutinied and sacked Rome in 1527.

Martin Luther had given Christian structure to the new Protestant Church, but the spirit of lawlessness also had been released. The warfare between Catholics and Protestants continued for generations to come.

Teshuvah 1533: England

King Henry VIII of England was not looking for a way to get closer to God. He was looking for a divorce so he could marry a younger woman and have a male heir to his throne. When the pope, fearing the Spanish, who had provided Henry's first wife, refused to grant an annulment, Henry began looking for alternatives.

Luther's Protestant movement had made deep inroads into England, and in the beginning, Henry had opposed it. Now, however, Henry decided to switch and embraced Protestants so that he could break with Rome and became head of the Church of England. In the Teshuvah eclipse year of 1533 he made the break, marrying a new wife and passing the Act of Appeals, which granted him supreme power over the English Church. He then set about reducing the power of the church by seizing the monasteries and forbidding contact between the priests and Rome. He wisely gave the monks a pension and set up the Archbishop of Canterbury as the highest ecclesiastical office so he would not be accused of hijacking the church. The net result was an English Church that claimed Protestant beliefs along with Catholic doctrine.

Henry also ordered that the English Bible be used in the churches, a major step forward in bringing the people closer to God. Thus, the Teshuvah invitation to return to God was accepted by many people. For those who rejected God's invitation to return, rough times were ahead, as England wavered for over one hundred fifty years between Protestant and Catholic visions for the nation.

TESHUVAH 1560 AND 1561: ENGLAND

Henry VIII died in 1547, leaving a frail, ten-year-old boy as the only male heir. During the boy's six-year reign, the Church of England adopted many Protestant practices. However, in 1553, "Bloody Mary" became queen and resolved to restore Catholicism. She martyred over three hundred Protestant leaders in only five years.

Elizabeth I came to the throne the year before the blood moon year of 1559. She wanted to bring an end to the bloody religious division and restore peace, thus accepting God's Teshuvah invitation to unify in Him in 1560 and 1561. In 1563, she adopted the Thirty-Nine Articles of Religion, which, while accepting many Protestant positions, were still appealing to Catholics. These articles saved England from the internal strife that had become rampant in Europe. However, the Pope, Spain, and France continued to be enemies of the English church and threats to the peace of England.

TESHUVAH 1560 AND 1561: THE VATICAN

The Catholic Church was slow to respond to the Protestant Reformation, partly because of political problems and divisions between Catholic kings and partly as the result of inertia and fear of change. Finally, Pope Paul III called the Council of Trent to deal with the issues raised by the Protestants. The sessions occurred in 1545–1547, 1551–1552, and 1562–1563.

The Teshuvah periods of 1560–1561 presented the option of returning to the unity of Christ and believers. Indeed, at some of the earlier sessions, Protestants had been allowed to attend. However, instead of seeking compromise, the Council of Trent decided to reject all of the issues and reforms of the Protestants. The council widened the gap between Protestants and Catholics, leading each to regard the other as an enemy of the faith.

It was not until the Second Vatican Council, also known as Vatican II, four hundred years later, that the walls started to tumble down.

Teshuvah 1571: France

French Protestants, known as Huguenots, were viciously persecuted by King Henry II until he died in a jousting accident in 1559, a premature death that many saw as the grace of God. His three sons each ruled for a time but were ineffective, as Protestants and Catholics fought a bloody civil war. In the midst of the war, in the year of the Teshuvah call to unite with God, the queen mother tried to arrange peace between the Huguenots and Catholics through a marriage.

Things went horribly wrong as the queen mother and her son, King Charles IX, rejected Christian unity. Instead of a celebration, they ordered the murder of Huguenot leaders who had gathered for the wedding. This brutal act, known as the St. Bartholomew's Day Massacre, led to renewed warfare. Because the chance for reconciliation was lost, bloody war consumed France until 1593.

Teshuvah 1589: Spain

Due to the Spanish Inquisition, the Protestant Reformation made little impact on Spain. Instead, Spain led the fight against Protestants. King Charles V tried to kill Martin Luther, and the Spanish fought Protestants in Germany, France, and the Netherlands. But a special animosity toward England existed, because Henry VIII's spurned first wife was the aunt of Charles V. Spain wanted desperately to take back England for Catholicism.

England and Spain maintained low-level conflict, sometimes breaking into warfare, until 1587, when Queen Elizabeth executed Mary Queen of Scots for her participation in a Spanish plot against England. An outraged Philip II, king of Spain, devised a plan to destroy England. In 1588, the Spanish fleet of one hundred seventeen warships known as the Spanish Armada set sail to pick up the Spanish army in the Netherlands and invade England.

The English Royal Navy fought bravely but had little impact. The weather intervened in their favor, and the armada lost many ships and two-thirds of its men. Queen Elizabeth gave glory to God and even wrote a hymn of praise. King Philip II admitted it was God who had defeated his Armada.

As the Teshuvah season came and went in 1589, Philip had the chance to repent of his attacks on England and to reconcile in Christian unity. Although he attributed his defeat to God's intervention, he refused to reconcile with the English. Instead, he began building a new armada in 1589. In fact, he built two armadas. One was destroyed by storms in 1596, and the second was driven back by storms in 1597. Philip died in 1598, having struggled with God, and missed the possibility to reconcile with his English brothers. Like Philip, the nation of Spain never recovered from God's judgment of destruction on its armada and started its long decline as a world power.

TESHUVAH 1598: FRANCE

In 1585, a bitter, three-way civil war broke out in France between the monarchy, a Catholic faction, and a Huguenot Protestant faction. Against superior forces, the Huguenot, Henry of Navarre, who was the crowned king of France, defeated the combined Spanish and Catholic forces arrayed against him. He was baptized Catholic but raised in the Protestant faith. Then he besieged Paris but found he could not take it. Finally, in 1593, he broke the stalemate by becoming a Catholic and thereby accepting the surrender of Paris.

Whether his Catholic conversion was sincere or not, Henry had bridged the gap and brought peace to the Protestants and Catholics of France. During the Teshuvah repentance season of 1598, he remembered the St. Bartholomew's Day Massacre and issued the Edict of Nantes, which granted freedom of religion in France. However, in 1610, he was assassinated by a fanatic Catholic. Known as Good King Henry, he had been the target of twelve assassination attempts because of the struggles between the Protestants and the Catholics.

The Edict of Nantes was a step in the right direction that, to the great cost of France, was revoked by King Louis XIV in 1685.

℘   ℘

By the end of the sixteenth century, the Protestants and Catholics had reached a point of stalemate within and between the countries of Europe. Unfortunately, neither side wanted to respond to Christ's prayer in John 17 that His believers be united. Another bloody century of religious warfare lay ahead for the broken body of Christ.

CHAPTER 4
TOLERATION

THE APOSTLE PAUL could have been writing to seventeenth century Christians when he wrote, "Accept the one whose faith is weak, without quarreling over disputable matters" (Rom. 14:1). He knew Christians would have many doctrinal differences. He knew it is common for people to assume themselves strong in the faith and those with differing opinions weak in the faith; however, he urged believers—whatever side they may be on—to tolerate others. Paul prayed for Christians to have a spirit of unity and accept one another to bring praise to God (Rom. 15:5–7).

Paul also urged Christians, "Let us stop passing judgment on one another" (Rom. 14:13). But Europeans of the seventeenth century were too bitterly divided to follow Paul's admonition. They did not understand that judgment begets judgment (Luke 6:37). As a result, millions would die as Christians wound their way through the century and finally, exhausted by warfare, began moving toward Paul's wisdom of tolerance.

TESHUVAH 1607 AND 1608: VIRGINIA

In 1608, a Teshuvah eclipse passed over the newly formed English colony of Virginia, offering repentance to an enterprise that had gone terribly wrong.

We also owe a great debt to Christian historians like Peter Marshall and David Manuel, authors of the classic *The Light and the Glory*, who have shown that God had a plan to form the United States as a Christian nation[1]—one that would embody the principles of toleration, acceptance, and unity among Christians, described by the apostle Paul in his letter to the Romans. We owe the authors a debt for exposing the roots of the Virginia colony as a presumptive business venture that never sought God's plan.

In the blood moon year of 1606, a group of English adventurers sailed to America expecting to find gold and riches and with plans to establish a settlement and exploit Virginia as the Spanish had done a century earlier in the New World. In the Teshuvah year of 1607 they settled on a malarial site called Jamestown and began looking for gold. They did not lower themselves to pursue activities like farming and fishing and were forced to trade with or steal from the native Indian population when their English provisions ran out. By time the Teshuvah eclipse passed over them in 1608, only thirty-four of the original one hundred forty-four adventurers remained alive.

Amazingly, the survivors did not repent and seek God. Instead, they and their English supporters doubled down, bringing in more "gentlemen" to look for riches. By 1624, only twelve hundred survivors remained out of the original six thousand who had settled in Virginia. A few returned to England, but the rest died of disease and starvation.

Nevertheless, God had a plan to redeem Virginia and use it mightily to form the Christian nation of the United States. But, we are getting ahead of the story.

TESHUVAH 1607 AND 1608: HOLLAND

In 1607 another band of Englishmen left home, but not for America—at least not yet. These were Christians who believed that the Church of England had lost its way and who wanted to worship God in their own congregations outside of the Church of England. Known as Separatists, they were considered a threat to religious orthodoxy. After the coronation of King James I at Westminster Abbey in 1603, the Separatists were persecuted and driven underground. They ultimately felt they had no choice but to leave their homeland and become refugees in Holland, where they were free to worship God.

Many felt they were called to Virginia, despite knowledge of the terrible suffering of the colonists there. As they prayed and sought the Lord, they did not receive a firm answer and had no financing for their journey. But with God delay is not denial, and the Separatists, who we call the Pilgrims, simply missed out on the judgments that fell on the godless Jamestown colony.

In due time it became clear that God did indeed want the Pilgrims to establish a Christian colony in America. With clarity, finances came to support the venture, and the first group of Pilgrims left Holland for America in 1620. The great adventure of God's plan to build a Christian nation in America was birthed and began to come alive.

TESHUVAH 1627 AND 1628: ENGLAND

In 1621 the Pilgrims landed in America. Unlike the Virginia gentlemen who came for riches, this group came to worship God freely. Like the settlers in Virginia, they suffered many losses in the beginning, but they managed to hold on and begin building a Christian society. Many Puritans in England who also wanted to worship freely felt the call to join their Separatist brethren in America but had vacillated because of the comforts of England and the risks of the New World.

The Puritans sought to purify the Church in England from all Roman Catholic practices. In the Teshuvah eclipse year of 1628, King Charles I turned up the pressure on the Puritans by appointing William Laud as the Bishop of London. He eventually became the Archbishop of Canterbury in 1633. An advisor to King Charles I, Bishop Laud had restored many Catholic doctrines and practices and at the same time tried to stamp out Puritan religious practices. Faced with this new round of persecution, many Puritans refused to compromise their faith. Instead, they accepted God's Teshuvah invitation to settle in America. During the sixteen years following 1628, some twenty thousand Puritans arrived in New England, solidifying the colony's survival.

As the Puritan exodus from England began, the colonizing company was reorganized to remove its government from the influence of the king and the English Church. The colony became an independent Christian Commonwealth, the beginning of a Christian nation.

TESHUVAH 1627 AND 1628: GERMANY

Religious divisions in Germany had come to a boiling point in 1618 when war broke out over the appointment of a Catholic emperor to rule Calvinist-controlled Bohemia. The war became known as the Thirty Years' War, as a string of conflicts arose between German Catholics, Protestants, and their allies. The first phase of the war, from 1618 to 1623, ended in defeat for the Calvinists because the Lutheran Germans and other Protestant nations did not support them. Following their victory, the Catholics began a ruthless persecution of Calvinists, revoking their religious rights and driving many into exile.

In the blood moon year of 1624 the German Protestants united and gained support from Holland, England, and Denmark. However, the new alliance suffered a series of defeats, and it seemed for a while that the whole of Germany might be conquered by the Catholic forces.

We do not know today what prayers went up from the suffering Germans in the Teshuvah years of 1627 and 1628. What we do know is that the Gustavo Adolphus the Great, king of Sweden, intervened in the war in 1628 and reconquered the lost Protestant lands in Germany by the time he died in battle in 1632. In 1635, the Peace of Prague restored the Protestant lands, which had been lost.

The Thirty Years' War should have ended at that time, but French imperial ambitions kept the war going until the combatants exhausted themselves and signed the Peace of Westphalia in 1648. Under the treaty, Lutherans, Calvinists, and Catholics were granted the equal right to worship. The principle of religious toleration finally came to Germany, but only after thirty years of brutal warfare and the loss of millions of lives.

Teshuvah 1644 and 1645: England

In the blood moon year of 1642, a civil war broke out in England with supporters of the king and the Church of England on one side and the Parliament and Puritans on the other. The persecution of the Puritans by the Church of England had created a backlash, which ultimately led to the war.

During the Teshuvah years of 1644 and 1645, the Puritans won a series of battles that ensured they would be victorious. The Puritans were also given the opportunity to allow everyone the freedom of religion that had been denied to the Puritans.

Sadly, the Puritans proved to be even more intolerant than the Church of England. The population of England was opposed to the new Puritan religious system, and the Puritans themselves were divided. Some, however, thought the reforms were not strict enough, and a second civil war broke out. When it was all over, the king had been executed and the Church of England abolished.

But the people still lived under the intolerance of an unforgiving religious system, and more conflicts were yet to come.

Teshuvah 1654 and 1655: England

In the blood moon year of 1653, Oliver Cromwell, head of the victorious Puritan armies, was given dictatorial powers by his supporters. Cromwell was a Calvinist who strongly believed that social problems came from individual sin. He also believed that Christians could be found in all denominations and, in theory at least, supported toleration.

On August 12, 1654, a Teshuvah eclipse passed over England, a sign and a warning to the nation to repent of its intolerance. No changes were made, and in the next year a royalist rebellion took place. The rebellion was easily put down, but Cromwell was displeased that the common people had not risen in his support. Convinced that a revival and return to God was necessary, he appointed military governors to force the local population to change their ways. Instead of forced revival, he received backlash and became more dictatorial, ultimately discrediting his cause.

Cromwell missed his chance to bring toleration and revival to England. After his death, the son of the king he had executed, Charles II, was welcomed back as king, and the Puritan laws and reforms, good and bad, were wiped away. Toleration in England would have to wait for another generation.

TESHUVAH 1672, 1673, AND 1674: NEW ENGLAND

By the blood moon year of 1671, the Christian colony in New England had survived its early challenges and become prosperous—so prosperous, in fact, that many had forgotten it is God "who gives the ability to produce wealth, and so confirms his covenant" (Deut. 8:18).

During the Teshuvah years of 1672 through 1674, the pastors in New England had seen a marked decrease in church attendance. For all of their preaching and entreaties, the people remained complacent and self-satisfied. But complacency in the vanguard of God's kingdom, as New England was, only opens the way for Satan to mount an attack. The settlers were deaf to the warnings of God and blind to the rising animosity and growing unity of the native Indian tribes.

A Native American Indian leader, Metacomet, adopted the English name King Philip in honor of a previously friendly relationship that his father had with the original Mayflower Pilgrims. However, he became concerned about the consistent Pilgrim infringement into additional land, and he secretly joined with other Indian tribes in a bid to destroy the colony. In 1676, Metacomet started the rebellion, called King Philip's

War, when he mounted an attack that took the complacent communities completely by surprise. Hundreds perished, and panic replaced complacency.

Prayer meetings were held seeking God's deliverance. Soon, everyone in the colony joined in repentance and prayer. God heard their prayers and brought about the defeat of King Philip. We can all learn the lesson about the dangers of complacency.

Teshuvah 1691 and 1692: England

The complacency that infected the Puritans in New England seemed also to reach the English as James II took the throne in 1685. As governor of Scotland in the early 1680s, he ruthlessly persecuted Scottish Christians who worshiped outside of the Church of England, but the English leadership seemed unconcerned. After he became king he revealed his agenda of returning Catholicism to power in Protestant England. The Protestant English, horrified at the thought of persecution and more religious wars, asked the Protestant William of Orange, the next in line to the throne, to become their king in 1688.

In the blood moon year of 1689, Parliament and the king passed the Act of Toleration. Though it only extended toleration to non-Anglican Protestants, it laid the groundwork for religious freedom.

Progress toward tolerance in England had come after the French king denied religious liberty in 1685 by revoking the Edict of Nantes. The French took up the cause of James II, offering him support and refuge. James II was finally defeated at the Battle of the Boyne in Ireland in 1690. Thereafter, in the Teshuvah years of 1691 and 1692 and beyond, France and England waged intermittent warfare until the French Revolution overthrew the Catholic dynasty in 1789.

Through their intolerance, the French weakened their country, driving out the Huguenots, some of their most productive citizens. The tolerant English, in contrast, received some of the blessings of unity and began to overtake the French as a world power.

TESHUVAH 1701: ENGLAND

In 1700 the King of Spain died, leaving his kingdom to a relative of the French king Louis XIV. The king of France then decided he could create an alliance of the two greatest religiously intolerant kingdoms in Europe and could bring Europe under his control.

Apparently England, Holland, and other tolerant countries spent the Teshuvah year of 1701 deciding what to do about the threat to religious liberty and their national security. War broke out the next year and came to be called the War of Spanish Succession. Historians cannot account for the amazing success of the English forces against the French, but we suspect that prayer had a role in the outcome.

The most significant battles were fought by 1704, three years after the Teshuvah year, but the war did not end until 1713. The French were soundly defeated, and religious toleration had survived its first international attack.

ஐ ௧

With the end of the War of Spanish Succession in 1713, the era of religious warfare in Europe came to a close. The division of Europe into Protestant and Catholic camps had stabilized, and the nations began focusing more on their national interests than their religious preferences.

The concept of only one church being allowed within a country also started to weaken. By 1713 it was recognized in the Protestant countries that religious tolerance and freedom of conscience damped down costly religious controversies.

The benefits of tolerance as a national unifier and blessing were only beginning to be understood.

CHAPTER 5

UNITY IN DIVERSITY

THE BIBLE SPEAKS of unity as something that is "good and pleasant" (Ps. 133:1), and in unity, "The LORD bestows His blessing" (Ps. 133:3). Jesus prayed for Christian unity: "So that they may be brought to complete unity. Then the world will know that you sent me" (John 17:23).

For two hundred years after the Protestant Reformation, the churches tried to achieve unity by force. Countless martyrs, both Protestant and Catholic, were created by wars and persecution. The only unity achieved was the unity of the grave.

By the early seventeenth century the nations began to appreciate the benefits of tolerance but were unable to find a way to realize the promised benefits of Christian unity. They have not yet learned that unity is not the same as uniformity. To quote Pope Benedict XVI, "We should first try to find unity through diversity, in other words, to accept what is fruitful in our divisions, to detoxify them, and to welcome the positive things that come precisely from diversity."[1]

In the eighteenth century Christians took their first halting steps toward unity in diversity.

TESHUVAH 1710: ENGLAND

In the blood moon year of 1707 the English took a small step toward unity. It was not a unity of churches, as had failed in the past. Instead, it was a unity that brought people with diverse churches together in political unity. In that year, the nations of Scotland and England united in a move calculated to bring blessings from unity in diversity of the Scottish Church and the English Church.

The Teshuvah year of 1710 would have been a time to pray for unity, and only a few years later the test of unity came when British Queen Ann died. She was the last of the Scottish Stuart dynasty, and the French used the son of the deposed Stuart King James II to stir up a rebellion in Scotland. Scotland did not widely support the rebellion, known as the Jacobite Rebellion, because of the benefits of the union with England and was quickly defeated.

Unity in diversity had passed its first test.

Teshuvah 1737, 1738, and 1739: Thirteen Colonies

In the blood moon year of 1736, the thirteen American colonies were a patchwork of religious beliefs. Puritans gathered in Massachusetts; Quakers, in Pennsylvania; Anglicans, in Virginia; and Catholics, in Maryland. Many other denominations were represented, and quite a few Americans had no religion at all.

To reach this diverse group of people God had to send something that would transcend their religious communities. This transcendent move of God, where people of all denominations follow the Teshuvah path of repentance and return to God, changes entire cities, religions, and nations and is something we call revival. The first such revival, known as the Great Awakening, began in the Teshuvah eclipse years of 1737, 1738, and 1739.

The revival actually originated in England, where John and Charles Wesley, along with George Whitfield, began holding large outdoor meetings to bring people back to Christ. Whitfield moved to the thirteen Colonies in 1739 and preached from Georgia to New England. Whitfield preached the same message to all denominations, including Presbyterians, Congregationalists, Anglicans, Catholics, Quakers, Puritans, and Moravians. Whereas prior reformers had tried to form new, pure denominations, Whitfield wanted his followers to reform the denomination they were in. Whitfield was the first to unite the Christians in the diverse denominations in Christ.

The Great Awakening brought tens of thousands to Christ across the thirteen colonies and began to unify them in their diversity.

TESHUVAH 1756 AND 1757: CANADA

In the blood moon year of 1754 a young Virginian named George Washington fought a losing battle with French forces in the disputed territory west of Virginia. This skirmish led to a world war between the British and French known as the Seven Years' War in Europe and the French and Indian War in America.

In 1755 Washington served under English General Edward Braddock in the disputed territory. Foolishly using European military tactics, Braddock led his troops into an ambush by French and Indians fighting American style and was killed. The Indians also targeted George Washington, who had two horses shot out from under him and four bullet holes in his coat. Miraculously uninjured, he led the survivors in a fighting retreat. Washington credited God for his survival, and the Indian chief who had ordered him killed in the battle said later that the "Great Spirit" had protected him. Thus, God protected His chosen vessel to father His Christian nation.

In 1757, a Teshuvah eclipse passed over Canada, warning of the coming judgment. The French enjoyed early success in the war, and the thirteen colonies were in danger of losing their religious freedom if the French prevailed. But George Washington and his fellow Americans were praying people, and the tide of battle turned. The English conquered Canada and defeated the French worldwide.

The religious freedom of the Americans was saved. As a bonus, the disputed French lands between the Appalachians and the Mississippi River, where the war began, were ceded to the British and would later be ceded to the Americans.

TESHUVAH 1766: THIRTEEN COLONIES

After the end of the French and Indian War in 1763, the English king decided that the colonies needed more taxes and less freedom. In 1765, King George III imposed the onerous Stamp Tax, which led Americans to take the position of "no taxation without representation."

The Teshuvah year of 1766 was a year of decision in the colonies, as they strove to protect their freedoms while remaining as loyal British subjects. The next year the king imposed a draconian tariff known as the Townshend Act. The Americans responded through petition and appealed to the king for fairness. In 1768, the Townshend Act was repealed except for the infamous tea tax, but regardless, the king sent two regiments of soldiers to Boston.

The Americans sought to peacefully protect their freedom, but the Lord hardened the king's heart, as he had with the pharaoh of Egypt over three thousand years earlier.

TESHUVAH 1775: THIRTEEN COLONIES

When a group of Americans dressed like Indians dumped a shipload of tea into Boston Harbor, it did not amuse King George III. In reprisal, he ordered his troops to close Boston Harbor in 1774. In April 1775 the British tried to disarm the colonial militia outside of Boston. They met on Lexington Green, where someone fired "the shot heard around the world," and the opening shot for the Revolutionary War buzzed through the air.

In the Teshuvah year of 1775, the Americans were forced to choose between fighting for their freedoms or submitting to the king's superior forces. Even then the Continental Congress petitioned the king to restore their rights, but the king hardened his heart and declared war on the colonies. Recognizing the dire threat facing the colonies, statesman Benjamin Franklin called for unity among the thirteen colonies, stating that, "We must all hang together, or most assuredly we shall hang separately."[2] The colonies did come together, unanimously issuing the Declaration of Independence in the name of a new entity: the United States of America.

America's Moses, George Washington, was selected in 1775 to lead the armies of the United States and free his people from pharaonic King George III. He also recognized the dangers facing the United States and designed the first flag of the new nation with a picture of an evergreen tree, memorializing the covenant with God, along with the words "Appeal to Heaven," recognizing his cause was hopeless without God's intervention.[3] The Americans were severely tested during the lengthy war. The leaders of America's churches called for the Teshuvah act of repentance and returning to God, and Washington himself called on his troops to honor the first day of national fasting in 1775.

God heard the appeal to heaven, and the colonies and the Christians held together, united in their diversity, and won their freedoms and the independence of the United States.

TESHUVAH 1784 AND 1785: UNITED STATES

In the blood moon year of 1783, the British and the United States signed the treaty granting American independence. The deliverer of America, Washington, could have declared himself a king or dictator. Instead, he resigned his commission, commending the new nation to God, and thought he would return home for good.

Almost immediately after the war, however, the unity that had secured victory began to dissipate. Under the Articles of Confederation, the national government had virtually no power, and the thirteen independent states began to draw apart. It appeared as if division would wreck the United States. So, George Washington responded again to the Teshuvah call to serve God and started a plan to bring unity to the country.

Washington's plan came to fruition in the Constitutional Convention of 1787, which he chaired. This time he took on the role of Moses, the lawgiver. The convention proved contentious and stood in danger of falling apart until Ben Franklin called for daily prayers to bring God into the deliberations. With God's help, the Constitution was adopted, and unity was restored to the United States.

The Convention also dealt with freedom of religion in the Bill of Rights. There would be no national church for the United States. Instead, the God-given right of individuals to worship in the diversity of their denominations without government interference was guaranteed.

The convention adopted the motto *E Pluribus Unum*, "Out of many, one," to reflect the foundation of the United States on unity in diversity.

TESHUVAH 1802, 1803, AND 1804: KENTUCKY

With independence, the United States gained a large new territory between the Appalachian Mountains and the Mississippi River. These lands, opened by a few pioneers before the Revolution, were flooded with settlers as Americans began the westward movement, which ultimately took America from sea to sea.

Churches were not established in the wilderness, and many of the rugged individualists of the frontier thought they needed none. They lived and died by their own strength, fought hard and drank hard, and even children drank watered-down alcohol. Those with families prided themselves on their self-sufficiency. Yet, it was upon those hard cases that God poured out His Spirit to start the second Great Awakening.

In the blood moon year of 1801, Pastor Barton Stone scheduled an outdoor meeting, called a camp meeting, at Cane Ridge, Kentucky. He participated in a camp meeting in western Kentucky the prior year, where ten thousand people attended. The twenty-five thousand who showed up for the camp meeting at Cane Ridge caught him unprepared. The Holy Spirit moved in power. Some came under conviction for salvation, others were slain in the Spirit, others gave testimonies, and yet others sang praises and worshiped God.

The crowds were so large that pastors could speak in different areas at the same time without interrupting each other. Denominational differences were ignored as Presbyterians, Baptists, Methodists, and other pastors preached messages of salvation. Attendees united in prayer and even sang the same songs. It became the first large, ecumenical meeting in history.

Pastors and participants throughout the United States carried revival away from Kentucky. In New England, Christians of different denominations joined together to establish orphanages, homes for the aged, hospitals, and benevolent societies. Christians began printing tracts and devotionals to distribute worldwide. The first foreign missionary society was formed, and Americans sent missionaries overseas.

Signs of the Christian revival followed the second Great Awakening. Citizens of Kentucky became Christianized, building churches and living Christian lives. Compassion for the needy moved Christians, and they provided for their care. Christians saw a lost and dying world and took the gospel of Christ to all nations because a group of pastors in the backwoods of Kentucky yielded to God's call for unity.

ℬ ℭ

Between the first and second Great Awakenings, God's plan to raise up a Christian nation came to fruition. He also showed the benefits of unity in diversity both in the political realm and in the spiritual realm.

Unity in diversity had shown the world that God sent Jesus (John 17:23), and many lost souls were converted in America. It was time for the United States to join the movements already under way in other Christian countries to take Christ to the nations.

CHAPTER 6
CHRIST TO THE NATIONS

BEFORE THE REFORMATION, the European concept of foreign missions consisted of conquest followed by forced conversion. This was also the strategy of the Muslim states. As a result, constant warfare occurred along their borderlands, from Spain to the Balkans. But neither side gained a decisive victory, and the Muslims blocked the expansion of Christianity. That changed when Europeans discovered gunpowder and oceanic sailing in the fifteenth century, outflanking the Muslims west to the Americas and south around Africa and into Asia.

Beyond the Muslim nations lay a world ruled by pagan god-kings and shamans. Their religions traced all the way back to ancient Babylon, which was described as the "mother of prostitutes" in the apostle John's vision of the woman on the beast (Rev. 17:5). John also spoke of "ten kings" who would arise and rule the world in the later times (Rev. 17:12). These ten kings, foreseen by John, were the European nations and their offspring, which controlled the world until the twentieth century. John went on to say that the ten kings would hate the Babylonian religion and bring it to ruin[1] (Rev. 17:16). The ten kings did this as they expanded their colonial empires and saw the overthrow of god-kings, shamans, and paganism in the Americas, Africa, and Asia.

The European nations were motivated by money and power, not a desire to spread Christianity. But, by destroying the pagan power structures, a door opened to allow the light of the gospel to penetrate into the kingdoms of darkness. Through that door went those called to warn the nations of the judgment to come and lead those who would listen on a Teshuvah-like journey of repentance and return to God.

It was Christopher Columbus, whose name means "Christ bearer," who paved the way.

TESHUVAH 1495 AND 1496: CARIBBEAN SEA

In 1496 a Teshuvah eclipse passed over Mexico and the Caribbean Sea, bringing a call to repentance to both the Spanish conquistadors and the native peoples.

During the blood moon tetrad of 1493–1494,[2] Spain had decided to adapt its conquest and forced conversion strategy, which had just been successful against the Moors in Spain, to the new lands discovered by Christopher Columbus. The conquest part worked brilliantly, but the forced conversion part failed to produce a vibrant Christian community. Nevertheless, the Spanish decision to conquer and convert the Americas was a monumental historic event that led to today's Christian population of eight hundred million in the Americas.

The Teshuvah eclipses of 1495–1496 brought the first indication that the conquest and forced conversion of natives in the Americas would not produce many lasting results. The Spanish force of twelve hundred men that left Spain in 1493 had conquered Hispaniola, an island in the Caribbean, and subjected its population, estimated to be three hundred thousand, to forced labor. Many of the indigenous Indians began to experience European diseases to which they had no immunities, causing as many as fifty thousand deaths by 1496. In 1495 a wave of despair swept through the island, and another fifty thousand Indians committed suicide. By 1508, the Indian population dwindled to sixty thousand, and in 1548, only five hundred Indians remained on the entire island. Even those who survived long enough to be "converted" quickly fell away according to the Spanish priest in charge of Indian evangelism. The forced conversion program failed, and when exposed by priests in the mid-sixteenth century, it caused a stain on the reputation of Spain.

The Spanish went on to conquer the Aztecs in Mexico in 1519 and the Incas in South America in 1532. Both nations participated in human sacrifice—fifty thousand per year in the case of the Aztecs—and so would have incurred the wrath of God (Lev. 20:1–5). The real conquest was attributable to European diseases, which spread rapidly and cut the Indian population in half ahead of the Spanish invasion. It is estimated that the North American native Indian population declined from 100 million to 5 million as the result of the plague of European diseases.

So, the first American Teshuvah call to repentance for the Spanish was ignored, causing great loss. Native Americans also ignored the Teshuvah warning, with tragic consequences.

Teshuvah 1542 and 1543: China

In 1542 the year of the Teshuvah eclipse over China, Portuguese Jesuit Francis Xavier set his sights on evangelizing the Far East and China.

Interested only in trade, the Portuguese did not adopt the Spanish policy of conquest and forced conversion. However, unlike many of his generation, St. Francis Xavier, a Roman Catholic missionary and co-founder of the Jesuit order, believed in conversion through love. He landed in the Portuguese trading center of Goa, on the western coast of India, bringing revival in 1542. Moving to southern India, he baptized hundreds at a time. He also sparked revivals in Malaysia, Japan, and other regions in Asia. His last mission was to take the gospel to China, but he died just off the Chinese coast in 1552. Others followed his example and brought Christianity into China soon afterward.

It is believed that Francis Xavier won one million people to Christ during his ten-year mission to Asia. The success of his mission showed the world that heartfelt conversion proved not only scriptural but much more effective than forced conversion.

Teshuvah 1607 and 1608: Canada

The colonial policy of the French in North America sat midway between the Spanish conquest policy and the Portuguese trading policy. Trading with the Indians, not conquering them, interested the French, as well as established areas of settlement for colonists as their trading posts became more prosperous.

In 1608, Samuel de Champlain, the Father of New France, established the city of Quebec as a trading post. De Champlain was more than a pioneer; he was a Christian strategist. Although he risked offending the Indian trading partners who kept his business going, he established a policy of sending missionaries out to convert the Indian tribes. Unlike the priests of New Spain, an army did not protect the missionaries from the Indians. Many of these brave Christians became martyrs.

De Champlain's missionaries penetrated deep into central North America. They reached Indian tribes from Nova Scotia, on the Atlantic Coast, to the Great Lakes and the upper Mississippi valley—all because a Christian leader risked his livelihood to spread the gospel.

Teshuvah 1719 and 1720: Moravia

At nineteen, Count Nicolaus Zinzendorf studied law in the Teshuvah year of 1719, but he decided to give his life to Christian ministry. He did not wait long.

Three years later he opened his family's estate to form a Christian community called Herrnhut, meaning "the Lord's Watch." The community kept watch while in prayer twenty-four hours a day, seven days a week, and became the longest-running Protestant prayer meeting in history, continuing for one hundred years. Their prayers kindled the fire of the Great Awakening and influenced leaders like John Wesley, who came to visit.

However, being watchmen for the Lord involved more than prayer. The Teshuvah scripture about the duty of God's watchmen to warn the sinner of the judgment to come (Ezek. 33) requires action. Zinzendorf saw the need for Christian missionaries and soon sent missionaries to the far corners of the Earth, prompting the first large missionary movement in history.

It proved to be one of the clearest examples of how prayer leads to revival and evangelism.

TESHUVAH 1784 AND 1785: ENGLAND

In the blood moon year of 1783, the Father of Modern Missions, William Carey, was baptized and began preaching in England. As he read and studied, he rejected the prevailing doctrine that evangelism ran counter to God's sovereign selection. Instead, he returned to the Great Commission commandment that Christians are to carry the gospel to all nations (Matt. 28:19–20).

Carey's understanding of God's desire to reach the nations ignited the fire for missions in him and others. He reorganized Christian missions by focusing on development of indigenous, local congregations and finding ways to make Christianity relevant to their society. As a missionary to India, he studied Hindu texts to gain insight into their thinking so that he could be more effective. He also oversaw a Bible translation project to bring God's Word to the people.

Perhaps Carey's greatest contribution to foreign missions was the concept that missionary work should be interdenominational. He invented what we now call the parachurch organization to bring Christians of various church affiliations together to support the cause of missions.

By uniting Christians in their diversity, he laid the foundation for the largest missionary outreach in human history in the nineteenth century.

TESHUVAH 1831: CHINA

It is said that Christianity came to China on a cannonball. It did so beginning in 1831. China saw missionaries from the Nestorian Christians in the Middle Ages and the Catholics following Francis Xavier, but government persecution greatly limited their impact. In 1724, the Chinese emperor outlawed Christianity but left open the port of Canton, now known as Guangzhou, as a trading facility for Europeans. In Canton, the English discovered a vast source of supply for the English addiction to tea. They also found a huge market for opium in China, which could be produced in India and traded for tea without the loss of any English silver. The Chinese tried to stop the opium threat, and the Opium War between China and England began in 1831.

When the war ended in 1842, England decisively defeated China, and the English forced the Chinese to give them Hong Kong and open five Chinese cities as treaty ports. Within these treaty ports Chinese law did not apply, creating what were essentially European colonies. The Chinese law against Christianity was also nullified in the treaty ports, allowing Christianity to follow the English cannonball into China.

Christianity breached the wall into China. The question yet to be decided was whether the coastal enclaves of Christians would reach Chinese society or be driven back like the Nestorians and Catholics were previously.

TESHUVAH 1840: CENTRAL AFRICA

In 1840, a young English doctor made the fateful choice to go to Africa as a missionary. That same year, a Teshuvah eclipse passed over central Africa, where he would become the most famous missionary of his age.

Dr. David Livingstone found the Africans to be unresponsive to the gospel but very willing to let him preach because of his medical skills. In that sense, he became the father of all medical missionaries. Even then, a chief who converted to Christianity fell back into polygamy, leaving Livingstone to look for another way to reach Africans.

His first efforts beyond his missionary work led him on several historic explorations of the inner parts of Africa. He came to hope that if these areas could be opened to commerce, the gospel would follow. He also found that Eastern Africa had as much slave trade with the Arabs as Western Africa had with the Americas, and began a fight to abolish it. Livingstone also fought against modern European racism, born of Darwin's theory of evolution, which saw Africans as inferior human beings.

Livingstone did not live to see his dreams for a Christian Africa come to pass. However, only a year after his death in 1873, the British and the Sultan of Zanzibar abolished the slave trade. Africans continued to resist modernization and Christianity, and as a result, the continent was divided between the European powers. Europeans showed little interest in evangelism, but they opened the continent to Christians, and by the end of the nineteenth century, twelve thousand British missionaries were following in Livingstone's footsteps.

Today, sub-Saharan Africa is one of the most Christianized areas on Earth. It is more Christianized than Europe. More Anglicans reside in Nigeria, the most populous African nation, than there in Britain.

TESHUVAH 1867, 1868, AND 1869: CHINA

In the blood moon year of 1866, Hudson Taylor sailed to China to lead the missionaries who joined the China Inland Mission, which he founded the previous year.

As a young missionary in Shanghai in the 1850s, Taylor felt that missions in the treaty ports run by the Europeans were not effectively reaching the Chinese. He followed the apostle Paul's admonition to be "all things to all people"

(1 Cor. 9:22) by adopting Chinese-style clothing, eating Chinese food, and living in the Chinese quarter. He became convinced that Christianity had to break out of the foreign enclaves and become Chinese if China was to be converted. Accordingly, he based the China Inland Mission in China and kept it independent of any denomination, using the powerful principal of unity in diversity.

The mission spread to all of China's provinces, and by 1895 there were more than six hundred missionaries in the field. Taylor's wisdom in building a Chinese church was vindicated almost a century later when the triumphant communists drove the foreign missionaries out of China in 1949. Instead of disappearing, as many had expected, Chinese churches survived and prospered. Today, over 100 million Christians reside in China.

℠ ☙

During the last five hundred years, the church has made a startling break out from its European base. As a result, Christianity continues to grow rapidly in former pagan strongholds like Latin America and Africa. China and many East Asian countries, while not majority Christian, have built vibrant churches. Nearly one-third of the world's population claims Christianity.

The great success of world missions came about as the church rejected the discredited conquest and forced-conversion strategy and returned to the biblical method of prayer for the lost, caring about their needs, and sharing Christ. The church also learned to tap into the power of unity by transcending the denominations in many cases and following the principle of unity in diversity.

CHAPTER 7

CALLING THE NATIONS
TO REPENTANCE

TESHUVAH IS NOT only a time for individuals to repent
and return to God. Nations are also called to cleanse
themselves from the curse of sin.

These curses include a long list of disasters, which come
upon those who disobey God's commands. Warfare brings
disease and starvation. Sin causes economic failure and decline.
Families are broken and children lost. The people are oppressed
and live fearful and unproductive lives. (See Deuteronomy 28.)

Teshuvah reminds Christians that Christ has broken the
curse, and God has shown us how to heal the nations: "If my
people, who are called by my name, will humble themselves
and pray and seek my face and turn from their wicked ways,
then will I hear from heaven, and I will forgive their sin and
will heal their land" (2 Chron. 7:14).

Nations rise and fall based upon their willingness to hear
the Teshuvah call to repentance.

TESHUVAH 1784 AND 1785: FRANCE

In the blood moon year of 1783, France seemed to be at the
apex of its power. It had just defeated its enemy, the English,
by supporting American independence and seemed to be
powerful and prosperous. Yet within six years the nation
collapsed into the chaos and terror of the French Revolution.

The foundations of the French nation had eroded for years.
Its church was rigid and intolerant, missing the blessings of
unity in diversity. The church disillusioned intellectuals, who
turned from Christianity to an anti-Christian philosophy
based upon reason. Lost in a pursuit of luxury, aristocratic
leaders failed to see the suffering and rising frustration of the

people. The American Revolution had opened a new hope of freedom from oppression.

The Teshuvah years of 1784 and 1785 afforded France an opportunity to repent and save itself. Instead, the nation ignored its problems until a famine led to rioting in 1789. The anti-Christian intellectuals quickly seized control of the country and overthrew the aristocrats. They then turned on the church, seizing its properties and driving forty thousand priests out of the country. Finally, they turned on themselves, instituting the infamous Reign of Terror. In the chaos, Napoleon Bonaparte gained dictatorial power, subjecting France to tyranny and the whole of Europe to years of destructive warfare. Ultimately, everyone lost; judgment fell on the church, the intellectuals, the aristocrats, Napoleon, and the people of France for a failure to repent.

The French wanted godless liberty, as opposed to the American model of liberty under God. They discovered that godless liberty is no liberty at all.

TESHUVAH 1821 AND 1822: MEXICO

In the year 1821 a Teshuvah eclipse passed over Mexico and Texas, bringing a warning of things to come.

As a Spanish colony, Mexico established an economic system, the encomienda, which sounded appealing, as it promoted a dependency relation system where the strong would protect the weak. In reality, it gave Spanish elites power and wealth gained by controlling the production and labor of the indigenous Indian population. A threat to that power came when imperial Spain adopted a liberal constitution to help in its fight against a Napoleonic invasion. Under this constitution, the special privileges of the elite would have ceased and equality under the law guaranteed.

The elites could have chosen the path of democracy and freedom, leading their people into a prosperous future similar to the United States. Instead, they did not repent of their greed and moved to sustain their power by starting the Mexican Revolution in 1821. A member of the elite and a military chieftain, Agustín de Iturbide, led the revolt, and by 1822, had made himself dictator of Mexico. The forces Iturbide unleashed brought instability and chaos for fifty years, with Mexico having fifty-two presidents between 1824 and 1867.

During a brief return to constitutional government in 1824, Mexico invited Stephen F. Austin to bring a group of Catholic settlers from the United States to populate the province of Texas. The promises of constitutional protections made to the Texans quickly evaporated, and twelve years later Texas declared its independence. After a series of defeats, including the famous stand at the Alamo, Texan general Sam Houston captured Mexican president and general Antonio López de Santa Anna and forced him to grant independence to Texas in 1836. Texas became a part of the United States in 1845, and a border dispute with Mexico led to the Mexican–American War in 1847. As a result of this war, Mexico lost its northern provinces, which today form the American states of California, Nevada, Utah, Arizona, Colorado, Wyoming, and New Mexico.

Today, the contrast between Mexican poverty and American prosperity is still painfully evident in border towns, all because of the elite's refusal to repent during the Teshuvah years of 1821–1822.

Teshuvah 1849 and 1850: United States

The ink on the treaty formalizing the American victory over Mexico in the blood moon year of 1848 had barely dried when the Americans were thrown into conflict over the issue of slavery. The new southwest territories were split between slave and free areas under the Missouri Compromise, which regulated slavery in the country's western territories. However, the State of California sought admission to the union in 1849 as a free state even though a large part of the state was in slave territory. This caused a crisis, as the Southern slave states feared that the Northern free states would ultimately use the votes of the free states to outlaw slavery. The debate then turned acrimonious, and talk of succession and war in Southern states was common.

Slavery had been a divisive issue in the United States from the beginning, as many Christians opposed the practice. In the early nineteenth century, more people in favor of abolishing slavery, known as abolitionists, were in the South than in the North. Gradually, however, most southern Christians were convinced to turn a blind eye to the evils of slavery, and they hardened their hearts toward their black Christian brothers. The controversy over California presented southern Christians with an opportunity to repent and begin to make a peaceful transition out of slavery.

Instead of repenting, the southerners supported the Compromise of 1850, which allowed California to be a free state and divided the Southwest between slave and free areas. In exchange, Congress passed the Fugitive Slave Act, which forced northerners to help southerners hunt down escaped slaves. This law turned many northerners against slavery as they witnessed the brutality of the slave catchers. After 1850, the country became polarized, and civil war became inevitable.

Since the southerners had refused to repent, God sent a great revival to the North in 1857, which led to an increased resolve to free the slaves. The Republican Party was formed in 1854 in reaction to the pro-slavery Kansas–Nebraska Act, which provoked open warfare in "Bloody Kansas." In 1860, Republican Abraham Lincoln won the presidency, and the next year the American Civil War broke out. Lincoln clearly saw the war as a judgment from God, requiring national repentance:

> *Whereas it is the duty of nations as well as of men to own their dependence upon the overruling power of God,*

> to confess their sins and transgressions in humble sorrow,
> yet with assured hope that genuine repentance will lead
> to mercy and pardon, and to recognize the sublime truth,
> announced in the Holy Scriptures and proven by all history,
> that those nations only are blessed whose God is the Lord;
>
> And, insomuch as we know that by His divine law
> nations, like individuals, are subject to punishment and
> chastisement in this world, may we not justly fear that
> the awful calamity of civil war which now desolates the
> land may be but a punishment inflicted upon us for our
> presumptuous sins, to the needful and end of our national
> reformation as whole people?[1]

The judgment was indeed calamitous. America's bloodiest war resulted, with over six hundred twenty thousand killed in battle. Approximately one white American had died for every slave left in bondage after the American Revolution.[2] In the end slavery was abolished, and the South was in ashes.

The curse of slavery, which the church could have dealt with in 1850, continues to haunt America to this day.

TESHUVAH 1886 AND 1887: GERMANY

In 1887, a Teshuvah eclipse passed over Germany, warning it to return to the God of its fathers.

It should surprise no one that the homeland of Martin Luther, who discovered that the righteous live by faith, would suffer spiritual attacks against its faith. As the religious wars of the sixteenth and seventeenth centuries faded into history, the German people became prosperous and complacent, losing their religious zeal. Beginning in 1787, German scholars developed a form of literary criticism that they used to create doubts about the truth and authority of the Bible. In 1878, Julius Wellhausen developed his documentary hypothesis, in which he claimed that the Pentateuch was composed much later than the time of Moses. This teaching, while at variance with much historic data, became accepted in German theological circles—as it still is in many liberal seminaries—and destroyed the faith of thousands of German Christians.

At the same time the faith of German Christians faded, the Prussians united the principalities of Germany into a German nation. The Germans developed an ideology that the state was the supreme object of devotion and the provider of all good things, replacing God. Under Kaiser Wilhelm I, the prosperous and liberal Germans became militant and expansionist. Wilhelm I won wars against Austria in 1866 and France in 1870 and called a conference in Berlin in 1886 that divided the African continent between the colonial powers. The German nation became the strongest power in continental Europe.

Like many European rulers, antiquities interested Kaiser Wilhem I. During a German archeological expedition, the excavation of the altar of Zeus at Pergamum in Asia Minor delighted him. This altar is widely believed to be the throne of Satan described in Revelation 2:13. Unaware of the spiritual significance of the altar, Wilhelm I brought the Throne of Satan to Berlin. The curse accompanying such an object, which sets apart the owner for destruction (Deut. 7:26), caught him unaware.

The curse first worked on the kaiser's family. His son, Frederick, would have been a good king but never ruled because he died of cancer three months after the kaiser died in 1888. His grandson, Wilhelm II, an immature, blustering, arrogant man who was unfit to rule, became kaiser instead. Under Wilhelm II, Germany became more militant and belligerent. He started a naval arms race with Britain and led his nation and Europe into World War I in 1914. The disgrace of a lost war drove Wilhelm from Germany in 1918. The destruction of Wilhelm I's dynasty brought the curse to all of Germany.

Had the church countered the curse in 1886, the son of Wilhelm I, Frederick, might have lived to be a wise king who steered his country on to the path of peace. As it was, according to an adviser to Wilhelm II speaking of Wilhelm's immaturity and quoting from Ecclesiastes, "Woe to the country that has a child for a king" (Eccles. 10:16, author's paraphrase).

Teshuvah 1914 and 1915: Russia

On August 21, 1914, a Teshuvah eclipse passed over Russia only three weeks after the outbreak of World War I. Russia received an earlier celestial warning in 1908 when the most powerful meteor strike in modern times hit Siberia. That meteor strike occurred as Russia agreed with Austria-Hungary on the annexation of Bosnia. Now the Russians were at war with Austria-Hungary and Germany as a result of the archduke of Austria-Hungary's assassination in the annexed territory of Bosnia.

The czar of Russia, and the nation as a whole, were not prepared for the war. Neither was the Russian Orthodox Church, which acted as a cheerleader for the monarchy. As disaster mounted upon disaster, the suffering Russian people began looking for answers outside the church and the monarchy. After millions had died, the czar abdicated, and a liberal government was formed in 1917.

The liberal government did not survive long, however, because the Germans had smuggled communist Vladimir Lenin into Russia in hopes that he would take Russia out of the war. An atheistic, anti-democratic manipulator, Lenin won over the masses by promising peace, land, and food. In October 1917 he forcibly overthrew the liberal government. At that very time, the Russian Orthodox Church conducted a spirited meeting debating about the color of their robes, totally unresponsive to the crisis.

Lenin made peace with Germany, but soon a bloody civil war embroiled Russia. True to his beliefs, Lenin had the czar killed, outlawed the church, and starved millions of Russians as he built a totalitarian, socialist government.

Because it did not repent and answer God's Teshuvah call, the persecuted church moved underground for seventy years.

Teshuvah 1932, 1933, and 1934: Germany

The defeat of the Germans in World War I did not bring repentance or an end to their suffering. Germany was forced to sign a humiliating, draconian peace treaty that created bitterness throughout the country. Financial depression wrecked the nation, and social order began to break down. By 1932, fear of a communist revolution wracked the German elites, and they looked for a strongman to restore order.

They thought they had found their answer in the leader of the National Socialist, or Nazi, Party, Adolf Hitler. Hitler preached a message of national restoration while his street thugs terrorized his opponents. He was virulently anti-Semitic and believed in a combination of paganism and pseudoscience, which today we call the New Age movement. In 1933, with the elites thinking they could control him and the church turning a blind eye, Hitler became chancellor of Germany. He quickly assumed dictatorial powers and created a ruthless police state to retain power.

By 1932, much of the German Protestant Church had become a faithless, powerless institution. Most had fallen for the "higher criticism" theologies that the Scriptures were not authentic and therefore not authoritative. Christ was viewed as simply a good man and sin considered a psychological problem. Hitler became sure he could control a Christless church, and for the most part, he was correct. Those like Dietrich Bonhoeffer and Martin Niemöller, who stood up for Christ, were sent to concentration camps with little protest from Christians.

This sad state of the church was described by Niemöller, who asked forgiveness even though he spent most of Hitler's rule in concentration camps, as follows:

> First they came for the Socialists, and I did not speak
>   out—
> Because I was not a Socialist.
> Then they came for the Trade Unionists, and I did not
>   speak out—
> Because I was not a Trade Unionist.
> Then they came for the Jews, and I did not speak out—
> Because I was not a Jew.
> Then they came for me—and there was no one left to
>   speak for me.[3]

As a result of German church's failure to repent and return to God, Hitler marched unopposed into World War II. Millions died in the war, and millions more Jews and others were killed in the Holocaust. The victorious Allies devastated and divided Germany. The church and the nation that birthed the Protestant Reformation experienced a tragic fall.

TESHUVAH 1952: UNITED STATES

When the Russians conquered Berlin, they took the throne of Satan to Moscow as a trophy, a fitting emblem for a totalitarian state bent on conquest. By the blood moon tetrad years of 1949–1950, the Russians had taken over Eastern Europe, China had fallen to the communists, and the United States was at war with Chinese troops and Russian aviators in Korea. But in 1949, God sent a man to bring revival to the United States and provide a Christian alternative to godless communism. His name was Billy Graham.

The year 1952 was a crucial test for the church and the Americans. Many American leftists and some Christians ignored the mounting evidence that Stalin was the biggest mass murderer in history up to that point. Others were manipulated by Soviet propaganda and wanted America to disarm even in the face of the Russian nuclear power. Still others were tired of the stalemated war in Korea. The American Christian values of freedom and tolerance were under attack at home and around the world.

In 1952 Americans and most Christians elected Dwight D. Eisenhower, leader of the Western armies that defeated Hitler, as president. Eisenhower turned to Graham for spiritual guidance and became the first president to be baptized while in office. The church, which had been sidelined for many years by liberal presidents, was brought back into the public square. Eisenhower began the National Prayer Breakfast and added the phrase "under God" to the Pledge of Allegiance. He ended the Korean War, leaving American forces to protect South Korea and its prominent Christian population, and strengthened our defenses at home and overseas against the communist threat.

In 1952 Graham held a crusade in Jackson, Mississippi, and saw that the organizers had intended to segregate the blacks from the whites. Segregation and the Jim Crow laws that supported it had been instituted in the nineteenth-century South as a backlash against freedom for slaves. Graham picked up the mantle of racial harmony and demanded that black and white Christians sit together, as they would one day in heaven. Under Christian pressure, the 1950s saw the outlawing of segregation in schools and progress toward racial equality. It took another Christian pastor, Martin Luther King Jr., to bring legal segregation to an end in the next decade and begin to heal the radical divisions in America.

Graham went on to preach the gospel in all fifty states and all six populated continents. He lived to see the discrediting and peaceful dissolution of Russian communism in 1989.

TESHUVAH 1961: UNITED STATES

From the beginning, God established the United States as a Christian nation. It was not to be a theocracy or to have a state church that would limit Christian expression. Instead, God instituted religious freedom and tolerance so that all

Christians could worship as their consciences demanded. The model for the church was the unity in diversity model founded in the union of the diverse states and seen in the great revivals and missionary activity of the eighteenth and nineteenth centuries. In the Teshuvah year of 1961 the average American Christian was blissfully unaware that the Christian foundation of America and our religious freedom was about to come under attack.

The battlefield chosen by the enemies of God was the United States court system, where secular elites and unelected judges could override the will of the people. Organizations like the American Civil Liberties Union began chipping away at the foundations. In 1961 the Supreme Court overturned a Maryland law that required state employees to express a belief in God. The church should have taken the Teshuvah warning and risen up, but it did not, and the floodgates opened.

In 1962 the Supreme Court struck down prayer in public schools. In 1963 the Lord's Prayer and Bible reading were banned. In 1973 abortion on demand was legalized, resulting in the murder of over 58 million babies. The courts became a battleground as Christians tried to fight back, but with limited success. In 2015 the United States Supreme Court mandated acceptance of same-sex marriage.

These anti-Christian decisions have had a devastating effect on the country. By removing God from our public schools, a marked decline in learning and morality has taken place, along with an increase in violence and crime. The decline in morality led to the 1960s sexual revolution, which has produced a tsunami of single mothers and poverty. Now the government has allowed sexually confused boys to shower with the girls, revoking girls' right to privacy. And the same-sex marriage decision has already opened the door for persecution of the church.

The United States stands in need of a great revival to redeem its godly heritage and the freedoms our forefathers fought for.

TESHUVAH 1979 AND 1980: IRAN

An authoritarian shah allied with the United States ruled the nation of Iran for several decades. Of all of the Islamic nations, Iran was the most tolerant of its Christian population, and its people were very westernized.

In the Teshuvah year of 1979, a group of radical Islamists arose, demanding overthrow of the secular government and creation of an Islamist state ruled by the Ayatollah Khomeini, a Shia Muslim religious leader. In Washington, DC, the Christian American president did not seek God but instead removed the shah and helped install the radical Islamist government. He was repaid for his foolishness when the radical government took the American embassy personnel as hostages in 1979. As a result, President Jimmy Carter lost the 1980 election.

The new Iranian leader let it be known the destruction of Israel was a top priority. As often happens, God confused His enemies in Iran and Iraq, and the two entered into a bloody war in 1980. Today, Iran is a totalitarian state with no freedoms and a nuclear program that threatens Israel and the United States.

Thousands of lives have been lost because of wars in those nations, and the people have suffered devastation, all because President Carter failed to seek God and support an ally in 1979.

TESHUVAH 1979 AND 1980: UNITED STATES

In the second half of the 1970s the United States appeared to be a nation in decline. The nation was deeply divided, and in 1976 Americans elected a president who was considered a Washington outsider to bring change. A born-again Christian, Jimmy Carter, continued to follow progressive policies, which produced results in America similar to everywhere else: economic malaise, inflation, unemployment, and stifling regulations. American foreign policy found itself on the defensive after the United States lost the Vietnam War, and as the United States faced ramped-up threats from Russia, which invaded Afghanistan in 1979. Weak-minded policies also led to the installation of a radical Islamist state in Iran, which held American diplomats as hostages.

Christians began to pray and seek God to bring healing to the land. God sent a deliverer, although not the man Christians expected. Ronald Reagan, a Hollywood actor turned politician, won the presidency in 1980. Reagan spoke of a new dawn in America and getting the government off the backs of the people. His free-market economic policies brought inflation under control and laid the foundation for twenty years of growth and prosperity. Hope had returned to America.

His foreign policy had one main goal: to destroy the "evil empire" of the Soviet Union. God brought Reagan two important allies in his struggle. The first was British Prime Minister Margaret Thatcher, known as the Iron Lady, who cleaned up the wreckage of Britain's failed experiment with socialism. The second was the head of the Catholic Church, Pope John Paul II, who had lived under the oppressive communist regime in Poland. With Reagan pushing high-technology defenses the Russians could not match, Thatcher's support in Europe, and Pope John Paul II's immense moral authority, the Soviets saw that they could not continue their evil, unproductive system.

Christians in Germany, Europe, and the United States began praying that the Russians would respond to Reagan's challenge to tear down the Berlin Wall. It happened after Reagan left office in 1989.

The Soviet Union fell not because of a war but because the people lost faith in the secular religion of communism. Never before in the world's history had a nation with the largest military force in the world laid down its arms and given back its empire. It is one of the greatest miracles of all time, brought about by the repentance and prayer of God's people.

TESHUVAH 1998 AND 1999: UNITED STATES

The smoke still rose from the ruins of the World Trade Center in New York as the people rushed to their churches in September 2001 to repent and pray for the terrible disaster. Yes, the terrorists could have been stopped except for bureaucratic infighting. Yes, Osama bin Laden could have been killed before the attacks, but President Bill Clinton became weak-kneed at the last minute. And yes, the foolish government policy of not protecting or arming airline pilots led to disaster. Those self-inflicted wounds were evidence of the failure to repent during the Teshuva eclipses of 1998 and 1999, when it could have made a difference. The failure to follow God's plan led to disaster three years later, as prophesied by prophet Chuck Pierce, and exposed the vulnerability of a complacent and arrogant nation.

In the aftermath of the 9/11 attacks, politicians and bureaucrats scrambled to avoid responsibility and avoid any mention of God's judgment on a sinful nation. They quoted from Isaiah 9:10 about rebuilding without understanding that Isaiah 9:10 was describing their very attitude of defiance against God.

Soon people quit going to church and returned to their normal routines. Even after the terrible judgment of 9/11, little repentance and no change occurred. The next judgment the nation brought upon itself couldn't be stopped.

TESHUVAH 2008: UNITED STATES

In 2008, a financial crisis second only in severity to the Great Depression struck the United States and the world. It was a call for Teshuvah repentance in the face of judgment.

The roots of the crisis reverted back to the Teshuvah eclipse years of 1998–1999, when the Clinton administration instructed the government-backed mortgage companies to relax lending standards to promote more home ownership. The relaxed standards led to a bubble in the housing market, as many people borrowed beyond their means to speculate on their homes. Wall Street firms got in on the act, and by the time the bubble burst, almost all of them were insolvent.[4] The government needed to provide liquidity to the markets to prevent a total economic collapse. In hindsight, however, the crisis could have ended in a few months with repentance and return to good economic policies.

But it was an election year, and few told the truth about the government's culpability. Instead, the election became a referendum on free enterprise and Wall Street. Christian intercessors sensed something was wrong and began praying for God's intervention in the election. But division in the Christian circles existed, as some supported the populist candidate solely because of his race. When the votes were counted, America elected its first black president, Barack Obama, and he promised to bring change to America.

However, the change he brought was unexpected by many. Higher taxes, increased regulations, and anti-business policies retarded economic growth, and average family income dropped. Climate extremism put thousands out of work, and only the productivity of America's oil and gas producers kept the Obama administration from making energy unaffordable for average Americans. Religious liberties were trampled to further the causes of abortion, gay marriage, and transgender politics, and lawless executive actions threatened the legal foundation of our freedoms.

Overseas, Obama ordered withdrawal of America's forces from Iraq in a precipitous manner, turning victory into defeat, and opened the door for the expansion of Islamist terrorism. He moved international security backward to the sphere-of-influence policies that started World War I, conceding influence to the Iranians, Russians, and Chinese. His centerpiece nuclear arms deal with Iran may set off a nuclear arms race in the Middle East. His apparent goal of dissolving the American superpower, and the peace it guaranteed, has made the world a much more dangerous place.

Amazingly, Americans re-elected Obama in 2012, and the judgment selected in 2008 continued. Now, more than ever, American Christians need to pray for revival and healing of their land.

ဆာ   ෬

The last two hundred years have seen the rise of an array of anti-Christian forces, including secularism, slavery, New Age religion, and a resurgence of Islam. These things are the result of church failures: failure to support human rights, failure to believe and follow the Scriptures, denial of Christ, complacency and compromise, and failure to seek God in prayer for His answers.

The church is called to make disciples of all nations (Matt. 28:19). It must lead the nations, and especially the United States, to answer the Teshuvah call to repentance before it is too late.

CHAPTER 8
CALLED TO JERUSALEM

I N MOST OF Judaism, the concept of Teshuvah and the city of Jerusalem are intertwined together. The Jewish understanding of the word *Teshuvah* is made up of two parts. The first part, *Teshuv*, literally means, "returning." The second part of the word is the letter *hey*, the last of the tetragrammaton name for God, *Jhvh*, which we translate as "Jehovah." Thus, the literal Jewish meaning of *Teshuvah* is "returning to *hey*."

The connection to Jerusalem arises because the *hey* in *Jhvh* represents the Shekinah, or manifestation of God's presence. In ancient Israel, the Shekinah resided at the temple. Many Jews believe that when the temple was destroyed, it fractured the *Jhvh*, and the *hey* went into exile. *Teshuvah* in this context means completion of the name of God by returning to a rebuilt temple in Jerusalem.

In the late nineteenth century God sent a prophetic stirring to His chosen people, the Jews, to make Teshuvah and return to Jerusalem and Israel.

TESHUVAH 1896: SWITZERLAND

In 1896 a young Austrian Jew named Theodor Herzl wrote the book *The Jewish State*, which became the manifesto of Zionism.

Herzl became concerned with the resurgence of anti-Semitism in Europe and looked for a way to protect his people. A secular Jew fully assimilated into German culture, he foresaw the day when assimilation would not be available to the Jews. He became convinced that a return to Israel served as the only answer.

Herzl organized the first Zionist Congress in 1897 in Switzerland and thereafter worked to obtain permission from the Ottoman Empire to establish a Jewish settlement in Israel. His request was denied, but Chaim Weizmann and Jewish leaders advocated simply moving to Israel and buying land without government approval.

By the time of Herzl's death in 1904, some thirty thousand Jews had made *aliyah*, meaning "ascent," to Israel. The dry bones were beginning to come together.

TESHUVAH 1914 AND 1915: BRITAIN

The outbreak of World War I brought the Zionists into the mainstream of international relations and paved the way for the establishment of Israel.

Chaim Weizmann, a Jewish scientist living in England, developed valuable war technology for the British government and gained favor for Zionism with high officials, including British foreign secretary Arthur James Balfour. For their part, the British looked for ways to encourage European Jews to support their cause. In addition, the British and the French developed plans to divide up the Middle East after the fall of the Ottoman Empire. To gain Jewish support for their cause, British foreign secretary Balfour wrote the famous Balfour Declaration in 1917, promising a national homeland to the Jews in Israel.

Later that year Britain took a step toward keeping its promise to the Jews when General Allenby took Jerusalem. With the Turks on the run, soon all of Israel fell into British hands. After the war, the League of Nations gave Israel to Britain as part of its Middle East mandate.

In 1921, the first fighting broke out between Arabs and Jews, as Arabs adopted a more hostile attitude. In response, the Jews began forming defensive organizations which grew to become the Israeli Defense Forces. Despite the opposition, the Jews kept coming.

By 1922, eighty-four thousand Jews lived in Israel.

Teshuvah 1932, 1933, and 1934: Israel

In 1933, a Teshuvah eclipse passed over Israel, a solemn warning of the danger coming to the Jews. Very few listened.

One of the Jews who listened was David Ben-Gurion. He understood that Hitler's rise to power in 1933 would lead to war and attempts to annihilate the Jewish people. In 1934, he said the Jews had only four or five years to escape from Germany before the war started. As a result of his efforts, some three hundred fifty thousand Jews were saved out of Europe before World War II began five years later in 1939.

The following Holocaust killed 6 million European Jews, about one-third of the worldwide Jewish population. We at the International Star Bible Society believe this event is described in the apostle John's vision of the fourth trumpet (Rev. 8:12), where a third of the sun, moon, and stars were struck. The imagery of the sun, moon, and stars here refers not to the heavens but instead refers back to Joseph's dream (Gen. 37:9–10) where the sun, moon, and stars represented the family of Israel; as prophesied in Revelation 8:12, one-third were killed in the Holocaust.

The magnitude of the Holocaust shocked the world and brought support for a Jewish homeland. In November 1947, the United Nations voted for independence for Israel, and on May 14, 1948, Israel declared its independence. United States president Harry Truman overrode his State Department and recognized Israel in eleven minutes. Favorable to the socialist aspect of Zionism, the Russians also recognized Israel immediately. But within three hours of the proclamation, Arab armies moved against Israel from three directions. In the first of several divine interventions, the Israelis stopped the attacks and even managed to hold on to a part of Jerusalem before the borders were settled.

The Mufti of Jerusalem, an Islamic cleric who had worked with the Nazis in World War II, urged the Arabs to leave the Jewish-controlled territories. In the new state of Israel lived six hundred fifty-five thousand Jews and only sixty-nine thousands Arabs. With a new flood of Jewish refugees from Europe and those fleeing from the Arab persecutions, the population of Israel reached one million by the end of 1949.

TESHUVAH 1970: ISRAEL

During the blood moon tetrad year of 1967, Israel won a miraculous victory over Egypt, Jordan, and Syria; reclaimed the West Bank of the Jordan; and most importantly, gained the entire city of Jerusalem. It took only six days, earning the name Six-Day War, and it became another great miracle worked by God for Israel.

Once again, Israel humiliated the Arabs. This time they continued sporadic, probing actions along the frontier with Israel. The Palestine Liberation Organization (PLO) joined in the attacks, but Israeli forces drove it back into the Jordanian mountains. Finally, after more humiliating defeats, the Arabs signed a cease-fire on August 8, 1970.

Israel won two great victories over the Arabs, and the temptation during the 1970 Teshuvah season was to become overconfident and complacent. Unfortunately, that is exactly what happened. As the Egyptians and Syrians prepared in secret for another war, Israelis relaxed their guard, believing themselves to be invulnerable.

The attack came on the last day of Teshuvah season, the Day of Atonement, in 1973, and was known as the Yom Kippur War. Most of Israel's soldiers were home for the religious holiday, and those on the front lines were pushed back by improved Arab weapons and tactics. At one point, only a handful of Israeli tanks stood between eight hundred Syrian tanks and the Sea of Galilee. But God intervened again, this time by confusing His enemies, and He saved Israel from annihilation. The overconfident Arabs abandoned their winning tactics. Israel miraculously recovered, and once more God rescued Israel from overwhelming enemy forces.

After this victory, however, the Israelis repented of their pride and increased their vigilance.

TESHUVAH 1979 AND 1980: UNITED STATES

During the Yom Kippur War, the United States had, for the first time, provided intelligence and material support at a critical time for Israel. After the war ceased, the United States became determined to prevent another war and initiated a peace process. Henry Kissinger negotiated a stable cease-fire between Israel, Egypt, and Syria. The president of Egypt, Anwar Sadat, made a historic trip to Israel in 1977 to seek a more lasting peace. The United States joined the initiative, and in the Teshuvah year of 1979, Egypt and Israel signed a historic peace treaty. President Sadat and Prime Minister Menachem Begin received the Nobel Peace Prize.

Following the signing of the peace treaty, both Egyptians and Israelites found it in their best interests to keep the peace. Tragically, the Muslim Brotherhood assassinated the Egyptian president in 1981, but his successors have honored the treaty. To this day, the Israeli border with Egypt has been secure. And because there is peace between Israel and Egypt, no other neighbor of Israel has the power to successfully attack it.

Unfortunately, new enemies arose at the same time to threaten Israel.

TESHUVAH 1979 AND 1980: IRAN

In 1979 the United States made a tragic blunder when it helped overthrow its ally, the shah of Iran, and allow a radical Islamic cleric to gain control of the country. Overnight, a progressive, prosperous, and tolerant nation became a totalitarian Islamist theocracy, ruling its own people through terror. Iran rewarded the United States for its naiveté by taking its embassy staff hostage for over a year. This Iranian government would not honor any law but its own.

The Iranians made no secret of their desire to destroy Israel. However, as He often does, God confused their minds, and they fought a war with Saddam Hussein's Iraq beginning in 1980. Israel found safety in the interim.

After his war with Iran, Hussein became involved with Islamic terrorism, offering a twenty-five-thousand-dollar bounty for families of suicide bombers. Hussein wanted to invade Israel, but God confused his mind, and he attacked his bankers, the Kuwaitis, in 1990. An American-led coalition soundly defeated him in 1991, and once again Israel was kept safe.

The Iranians returned to the game by supporting the terrorist group Hamas in Gaza and the Hezbollah terrorists in Lebanon. These groups have fired Iranian missiles at the civilian population of Israel and fought with Israel defense forces but have had no major impact.

Frustrated by their inability to strike a telling blow against Israel, the Iranians adopted another strategy for long-range warfare. They began developing a nuclear bomb and a delivery system.

TESHUVAH 2008: UNITED STATES

The American invasion of Iraq in 2003 succeeded in overthrowing the despotic Saddam Hussein, but in the aftermath, the Sunni and Shia Muslims mounted a deadly civil war. The civil war aroused domestic opposition to the Iraq War in the United States but had been almost extinguished at the time of the 2008 election in the United States.

Nevertheless, the Iraq War became unpopular, and in the presidential election of 2008, Barack Obama promised to end the war. He ended the war by prematurely withdrawing American troops, and Iraq fell back into chaos with Sunni Islamic State terrorists fighting Iranian-backed Shiites. Meanwhile, a civil war began in Syria with Iranian and Hezbollah troops supporting the dictator against moderate rebels and the Islamic State terrorists.

Unknown to anyone outside of his inner circle, Obama made a decision to withdraw completely from the Middle East, leaving it as a sphere of influence for the Iranians.[1] The policy also called for America to distance itself from its allies Saudi Arabia, Turkey, Egypt, and Israel. It was this disentanglement policy that led the president to push through the nuclear treaty with Iran, which most experts believe will allow them to complete the development of nuclear arms.

For now, the effect of the Middle East turmoil on Israel is positive, as God is using another of his favorite tactics to prompt Israel's enemies to fight among themselves. Only God knows what will happen next.

ॐ ॐ

In the apostle John's vision of the trumpets, we believe that the fifth trumpet (Rev. 9:1–11) describes a war between the Arabs and Israel. The Arabs do have a "star" which fell "from the sky to the earth" (v.1), a meteorite, in the center of the great mosque in Mecca. They are "told not to harm the grass...or any plant or tree" (v. 4) in the Quran. "The key to the shaft of the Abyss" (v. 1) refers to the Arab oil reserves. They will fight Israel but will not kill it, and the war will go on for one hundred fifty years, using a prophetic day-for-a-year interpretation. If this interpretation is correct, there will be one hundred and fifty years of warfare between the Arabs and Israel. We are yet half way through that war.

What we do know is that God moved on the Jews to make the Teshuvah move to Jerusalem. It was God who opened up the land and God who called them back to become a nation. God gave them Jerusalem and has protected Israel through every attack.

The miracle of Israel's rebirth is a sign of God's power and sovereignty for Christians.

It is also a sign that Christians need to make a Teshuvah journey back to God's presence, as the Jews made their Teshuvah journey back to Jerusalem.

CHAPTER 9
CALLED TO UNITY IN CHRIST

I N THE LATE nineteenth century the Jews felt a stirring to return to God's presence by returning to Jerusalem and the temple. At the same time, a desire to return to God's presence in the new covenant temple of the Holy Spirit within themselves stirred Christians. God called His church back to unity in Christ and prepared the way for the greatest revival in history.

TESHUVAH 1896: THE VATICAN

By the end of the nineteenth century, the Catholic Church, like the other churches, dealt with the deadening influence of attacks on Scripture from anti-Christian scholars and the rapid advances of the secular, anti-Christian worldview. The Catholic Church needed a new touch from God.

Pope Leo XIII realized that Christians needed a new Pentecost to bring revival. He looked back to the first Pentecost, when Christ commanded His followers to wait together in Jerusalem for the baptism of the Holy Spirit (Acts 1:4–5). After Jesus ascended to heaven, about one hundred and twenty believers returned to Jerusalem, as Jesus commanded, remaining constantly in prayer (Acts 1:12–14). Ten days later, on the Feast of Pentecost, the Holy Spirit came upon them in power, bringing the beginning of the church (Acts 2:1–6).

The pope established a novena, or nine successive days of prayer, duplicating the nine days prior to Pentecost when the believers had been united in prayer, and ordered it to be observed every year. The Catholic Church prayed for a new outpouring of the Holy Spirit and church unity during the novena.

It took over seventy years before the Catholic Church was prepared to have that prayer answered, but the prayer helped open the gates of heaven for the outpouring of the Holy Spirit on another group of Christians.

TESHUVAH 1896: UNITED STATES

In 1896 a young Methodist pastor named Charles Parham seeking the Holy Spirit decided to leave the denominational church in order to fully serve God. He began to hold meetings open to all denominations outside of the churches, believing for the Holy Spirit to manifest. Parham became known as the Father of the Pentecostal movement.

In 1897 Parham began praying for the sick after a son was miraculously healed from a serious illness. He became a healing evangelist and opened a home for those seeking divine healing. In 1900, he started a Bible school in Topeka, Kansas, for those of all denominations willing to study the Word and believe God. One of their assignments—the study of the baptism of the Holy Spirit—led to an outpouring of the Holy Spirit after the students all agreed that every instance of baptism in the Holy Spirit was accompanied by speaking in other tongues.

The students received the baptism at first, and then a group of local pastors. Only then, in January 1901, did Parham himself begin speaking in tongues. News of the new Pentecost spread quickly, and Parham traveled the country to invite people to receive the baptism of the Holy Spirit and healing. Thousands responded, and the modern Pentecostal outpouring started.

TESHUVAH 1905: UNITED STATES

In 1905 Parham opened a school in Houston, Texas. As always, it was non-denominational, but in addition Parham decided it should be interracial as well. In Parham's school a black man named William J. Seymour learned about the baptism of the Holy Spirit. He had not received it before he was called to preach at a Holiness church in Los Angeles in 1906. Unfortunately, when he expressed his views on Holy Spirit baptism he was immediately thrown out of the church that had called him to preach. But God had a plan for Seymour, and soon other Christians welcomed it, allowing him to begin leading home-based meetings. At one of these meetings, on April 9, 1906, people began to receive the baptism of the Holy Spirit and spoke in tongues. On April 14, 1906, Seymour rented the Azusa Street Mission, and the Azusa Street Revival began.

Non-denominational and interracial, the revival created a powerful, visible unity. The Spirit led the meetings, with prayers, speaking, or singing occurring spontaneously. Seymour encouraged speaking in tongues but did not require speaking in tongues, as some Pentecostals started to do. Instead, he said, "Baptism in the Holy Ghost and fire means to be flooded with the love of God and power for service."[1]

The revival meetings themselves were small, never larger than several hundred, but the influence of the Azusa Street Revival on the Pentecostal outpouring came through those who carried it to other places. People took the revival to other churches in Los Angeles, throughout the south and central United States, and into the big cities of New York and Chicago. Missionaries carried the movement to Europe, China, East Asia, India, South Africa, Egypt, Liberia, and Canada. At least eight Pentecostal denominations, including the Assemblies of God and Church of God in Christ, trace their roots back to the Azusa Street Revival.

The Azusa Street Revival's influence continues to this day. In 2016, the one hundred tenth anniversary of the revival marked the occasion of a large gathering in Los Angeles. Almost one hundred thousand Christians of all denominations and races attended the event, a call to prayer and fasting. The organizer, Lou Engle, founder of The Call movement, said, "Only a united church can heal a divided nation."[2] In a historic moment at that meeting, Engle and a group of Protestant leaders prayed with international charismatic Catholic leader Matteo Calisi[3] and representatives from the Catholic Diocese of Los Angeles for reconciliation and unity.

The Azusa Street anointing for revival based on unity lives on.

TESHUVAH 1961: THE VATICAN

The Teshuvah year of 1961 saw the factions of the Catholic Church, the traditionalists and the modernists, preparing for the most important Catholic meeting in modern history, the Second Vatican Council.

Pope John XXIII opened the council in 1962 with a prayer that harkened back to Leo XIII: "Divine Spirit, renew Your wonders in our time, as though for a new Pentecost."[4] It soon became clear a mighty wind blew through the Catholic Church, as the traditionalists lost control of the council and reforms were instituted in the Catholic Church. Changes were made in the church liturgy, allowing services to be held in the languages of the people, with more recognition of biblical giftings and involvement from lay people.

The church's relationship with non-Catholic Christians underwent radical changes. The concept of freedom of religion was endorsed, ending fifteen hundred years of opposition. In addition, the Catholic Church recognized the positive spiritual values and gifts of the non-Catholic churches. Thus, non-Catholic Christians were no longer considered heretical but were instead recognized as brother Christians. The church established an office promoting Christian unity and established ecumenical offices in the dioceses.

A change in the church's viewpoint on Pentecostalism became another reform of the Second Vatican Church. The traditionalists fought against recognition of charismatic gifts, but Cardinal Leo Jozef Suenens from Belgium prevailed, and the council held that the gifts should be welcomed in the church. This was a critical step forward in answering Pope Leo XIII's prayer for a new Pentecost.

Together, the ecumenical unity movement and the acceptance of the gifts of the Holy Spirit opened the way for one of the greatest revivals in the history of the church.

TESHUVAH 1970: UNITED STATES

During the blood moon tetrad year of 1967 a group of Catholics received the baptism of the Holy Spirit at Duquesne University in Pittsburgh. The experience carried to other places, and soon a charismatic revival among Catholics broke out. Thousands of Protestants shared the experience, and a worldwide revival began. This revival has produced 600 million charismatic believers.

The new enthusiastic, charismatic believers presented a challenge to the established denominations because they largely remained within their denominations, praying and spreading the charismatic revival. At first the small prayer groups of the charismatics were hardly noticeable, but by 1970 they became too large to ignore. The churches needed to decide how to deal with them.

Having accepted the idea of spiritual gifts in Vatican II, the Catholic Church quickly accepted charismatic Catholics. By 1970, a Catholic organization, the National Service Committee, organized to deal with charismatic issues. Some Catholic prayer groups wanted to organize themselves into covenant Christian communities, and these were allowed to be self-governing and self-funding under the authority of the local bishops. Over time, the covenant communities were allowed to be interdenominational, reflecting the ecumenical spirit of the charismatic Catholics.

Most of the mainline Protestant churches also accepted charismatic prayer groups, forming their own service committees based on the Catholic example. Some other denominations opposed the charismatics and forced them out. The huge Southern Baptist Convention adopted no official policy but occasionally ejected a charismatic church and did not permit charismatics to be missionaries until recently.

The culmination of this period of ecumenical charismatic growth came in the Kansas City Conference of 1977. Leaders of denominational charismatic groups agreed to meet together in unity to worship together. Some fifty thousand charismatics filled the football stadium to hear from prominent Catholic and Protestant leaders.

It was at that meeting that the scandal of division between Christians came to the forefront as Catholic leader Ralph Martin spoke and prayer occurred to heal the broken body of Christ:

> *Mourn and weep, for the body of my Son in broken.*
>
> *Mourn and weep, for the body of my Son is broken.*
>
> *Come before me with sackcloth and ashes; come before me with tears and mourning, for the body of my son is broken.*
>
> *I would have made you one new man, but the body of my Son is broken.*
>
> *I would have made you a light on the mountaintop, a city glorious and splendorous that all the world would have seen, but the body of my Son is broken.*
>
> *The light is dim. My people are scattered. The body of my Son is broken.*
>
> *Turn from the sins of your fathers. Walk in the way of my Son. Return to the plan of your Father, return to the purpose of your God.*
>
> *The body of my Son is broken.*[5]

Even so, after the great Kansas City meeting of 1977, the push for unity lessened, and it fell to another generation to heal the broken body of Christ.

It is no accident that in 2017 the pathway of the Teshuvah eclipse ran directly over Kansas City.

TESHUVAH 1970: UNITED STATES

In the blood moon tetrad year of 1967, something important happened in the Spirit when the Jews captured Jerusalem. In the Charismatic movement that began in 1967, large numbers of Jews became Christian. Yet, many of them felt unwelcome, as the churches were thrown into confusion by the phenomenon of Jewish Christians, and many of the new Christian Jews wanted to retain their Jewishness.

In 1970 God gave Jewish Christian leader Marty Chernoff a vision showing the words *messianic Judaism*. Here lay the answer to the dilemma of the Jewish believers. They could worship Christ in a messianic synagogue, similar to what would have taken place in first-century Israel. Understanding they were saved by grace, they could still worship God in Hebrew using a Hebrew Bible and a deep Jewish understanding of the Scriptures. They could be fully Christian and fully Jewish.

Messianic Judaism has made an enormous impact. The number of Jews who believe in Jesus the Messiah has grown from two thousand in 1967 to an estimated 1 million today. Messianic churches have been established worldwide, even in Israel. The gentile Church has benefited from the messianic insights into the prophetic meaning of the Feasts of Israel and the Jewishness of Jesus.

Even so, there is a segment of the church that has been slow to accept the messianic Jews. In response, a group of messianic leaders led by Marty Waldman from Dallas, Texas, have formed an organization to seek a second Jerusalem Council of the church. In the first Jerusalem Council, described in Acts 15, the Jewish church decided that gentiles could remain gentiles and still be admitted to the church. The Toward Jerusalem Council II movement seeks a Jerusalem Council where the Gentile church will agree that messianic Jews can remain Jews and receive recognition as Christians.[6]

Many Christian leaders believe that messianic Jews are a sign of God's end-times plan. They are certainly an essential part of the unity movement.

TESHUVAH 1998 AND 1999: GERMANY

The Teshuvah eclipse of 1999 passed over Germany and brought history to a full circle.

On October 31, 1999, the Lutheran World Federation and the Catholic Church signed the Joint Declaration on the Doctrine of Justification in Augsburg, Germany. In the declaration, Catholics and Lutherans agreed we are justified by faith apart from works (Rom. 3:28) and it is by grace alone through faith in Christ that we are saved (Eph. 2:8). They further state that, while doctrinal differences remain, the agreement on justification by God's grace through faith in Christ eliminates any doctrinal condemnation.

The five-hundred-year-old dispute between Martin Luther and the Catholic Church is resolved. The protest is over. The last paragraph of the declaration reads:

> We give thanks to the Lord for this decisive step forward on the way to overcoming the division of the church. We ask that the Holy Spirit lead us further toward that visible unity which is Christ's work.

TESHUVAH 2017 AND 2018: UNITED STATES

The end of the protest signified by the Joint Declaration on the Doctrine of Justification in 1999 did not bring an end to the divisions in the church, although it was a historic act of unity.

In the blood moon tetrad of 2014–2015, God gave a celestial sign to His church that He was again sending a great revival to the Earth.[7] Early in 2014 Pope Francis I entrusted a video message to a Protestant bishop from South Africa, Tony Palmer, to deliver to a group of Protestant pastors at a conference held by Charismatic leader Kenneth Copeland.[8] It was a historic message of brotherhood, love, acceptance, and yearning for unity. No pope had ever spoken like that before, and this message, we believe, opened the door for a great revival based on Christian unity and evangelism, as Jesus prayed in John 17.

Pope Francis was no stranger to Christian reconciliation. In 2003, Catholic charismatic leader Matteo Calisi persuaded him to hold Christian reconciliation meetings in Buenos Aires, where he was cardinal. Those meetings grew to involve thousands of priests and pastors, bringing a spirit of unity where conflict arose. It was in Argentina that Pope Francis became a mentor to Calisi's co-worker Bishop Palmer, who delivered Francis's reconciliation message to Copeland. As cardinal, he also established relationships with the messianic Jews, and the last person who prayed for him as he left his office for the papal selection meeting was messianic leader Marty Waldman.

As pope, Francis has received dozens of Christian leaders from all over the world and especially from the United States. Copeland organized a meeting in response to the Pope's video that included John Arnott, James Robison, and several others. Some American leaders, like Joel Osteen, have met separately with Pope Francis, while many have attended meetings with groups of leaders. Pope Francis has encouraged dialogue at these meetings and, for example, lay to rest a false rumor that he was a universalist in a conversation with International House of Prayer leader Mike Bickle.

The 2017 Teshuvah eclipse, with its path across America, tells us that this international reconciliation between leaders must be brought down to the national and local levels in the United States if we are to realize the life-changing power of the unity revival signified by the blood moons. In 2016, Christian unity was featured in the Azusa Now meeting in Los Angeles; the Together 2016 event in Washington, DC, where the pope sent a video; and the 2016 Kairos meeting in Augusta, Georgia. A Kairos meeting was scheduled in 2017 in Kansas City for the expressed purpose of bringing national and local leaders together to take the unity revival to the national and local levels.[9] But local unity movements, like the ones in Phoenix and Houston, are few, and much more must be done to bring the church to unity and revival, as Jesus prayed in John 17.

Teshuvah 2017 is shaping up to be a year of destiny for individuals, the church, and the nation. More than ever, we need to respond to God's Teshuvah invitation to repent and return to Him.

PART III

RESPONDING TO TESHUVAH 2017

This day I call the heavens and the earth as witnesses against you that I have set before you life and death, blessings and curses. Now choose life, so that you and your children may live and that you may love the LORD your God, listen to his voice, and hold fast to him. For the LORD is your life.
—Deuteronomy 30:19–20

CHAPTER 10
REVERSING THE CURSE

T HE TRUTH IS, every person must make a Teshuvah journey to return to God. The only way to reverse the curse of sin and death is to repent, return to God, and live in His presence.

Jesus had to make the Teshuvah journey to overcome temptation and leave Satan with no hold on Him (John 14:30). It happened during His forty days of temptation (Matt. 4:1–11), which many scholars date to late summer of AD 26, the Teshuvah season leading up to the Day of Atonement. As an observant Jew, Teshuvah became the prescribed time for Jesus to go on a forty-day fast.

After forty days, Satan appeared to Jesus and presented Him with three sets of choices, choices we all must make. Jesus responded with passages from God's Word, and since both Jesus and Satan are Bible scholars, the context of those passages further solidifies Jesus's answers.

To cut off the devil's hold on us and reverse the curse, we must give the same answers Jesus did.

DOUBT OR FAITH

Satan first asked Jesus to turn the stones into bread, questioning to see if Jesus knew who He was and if He trusted in God's provision for His needs. Many of us have the same doubts, not knowing we are called to be children of the King and wondering if God will take care of us. This doubt served as the source of Martin Luther's torment, as he tortured himself in guilt and condemnation trying to earn a position with God that he already had.

The answer Jesus gave about not living by bread alone came from Deuteronomy 8:1–5. The passage begins with God's promise to bring us into the place of His promise if we are obedient, so we that know God has good plans for us. God next reminds us of our desert experience, how He humbles us to test us so we will know what is in our heart.

God humbles us, even allowing us to be needy, but then He sends His provision. He does this to teach us that, "Man does not live on bread alone but on every word that comes from the mouth of the LORD" (Deut. 8:3). The Lord then reminds us He has met our needs on our journey. Finally, He assures us that throughout it all He is our loving Father when He says He disciplines us as a father would discipline his child.

The answer to our doubts is to know we are God's children and to have faith in a God who has good plans for us, leads us by His voice, provides for us, and loves us as our Father. For Martin Luther, this revelation came from Romans 1:17: "The righteous will live by faith." This freed him from doubt and fear of his standing with God and loosed him to pursue his destiny. It can be the same for us.

> *Therefore, there is now no condemnation for those who are in Christ Jesus, because through Christ Jesus the law of the Spirit who gives life has set you free from the law of sin and death.*
>
> —ROMANS 8:1–2

Choose faith to reverse the curse.

TEST GOD OR OBEY HIM

Satan next asked Jesus to perform a presumptive act of jumping off the temple, even giving Him a scripture, questioning again who He was, and urging Him to test God's protection. Many Christians have fallen into the trap of presuming God's blessing without really following Him, to their great loss.

King Philip II of Spain admitted that it was God who had destroyed the Spanish Armada in 1588, but he presumed God's blessing, thinking he was doing God a favor, and built two more armadas, which God destroyed. The Jamestown settlers came for gold, not God, and 80 percent of them died because they had presumed on God. Southern slave owners built their fortunes on stolen slave labor and saw their presumption turn to ashes as their fortunes were destroyed and many died in the Civil War.

Jesus warned us not to fall into presumption by saying, "Do not put...your God to the test" (Deut. 6:16). The rest of the story, continued in Deuteronomy 6:17–26, reminds us that God expects us to obey Him if we are to receive His promises and overcome our enemies. The commands of God are for our own good. If we follow them, we will prosper and be kept alive.

Obedience to God is the answer to our urge to presume on God. God wants our obedience not because failure will condemn us, since those in Christ are not condemned, but to save us from harm. King Philip could have saved many lives and much grief if he obeyed God and made peace. Jamestown could have prospered with little loss of life if the settlers sought God's purpose for their colony. The southerners could have kept their fortunes and lives if they repented and freed their slaves voluntarily.

Teshuvah tells us that even when we have sinned and presumed on God, we can repent and return to Him. Look at the Puritans, who suffered an Indian war because they quit following God. Once they belatedly made the Teshuvah journey of repentance, the Lord sent them victory, and peace returned. We may suffer crushing losses because of our disobedience, but God is ready to forgive us and restore us as we repent and reverse our sinful actions (1 John 1:9).

Choose obedience so you can live and prosper.

SELL OUT OR SERVE GOD

Satan came down to his last card with Jesus. Jesus knew God was His Father and had faith. He also knew not to test God or there would be bad consequences. Only bribery remained. Since Jesus was such a big fish, Satan offered Him everything he had, the whole world, if Jesus would sell out to him. For the rest of us, the offer price is much lower. Jesus did not take the bait, and neither should we.

Some of us have comfortable careers to consider, like George Whitfield, Charles Parham, or Martin Niemöller. Hollywood offered Billy Graham a million-dollar contract to leave his crusades. Others, like Henry of Navarre, had kingdoms at stake. And still others, like the Pilgrims and Dietrich Bonhoeffer, risked their own lives to remain loyal to Christ.

Jesus simply replied, "Away from me, Satan! For it is written: 'Worship the Lord your God, and serve him only'" (Matt. 4:10), quoting a portion of Scripture taken from Deuteronomy 6:4–15. This passage contains what Jesus called the greatest commandment: "Love the LORD your God with all your heart and with all your soul and with all your strength" (Deut. 6:5). The Lord also warned us that if we quit loving Him, if we sell out, then we are on the road to destruction.

It was the love of God that led Whitfield and Parham to launch out with a message from God. Love of God caused Billy Graham to turn down a fortune and led the Pilgrims, Niemöller, and Bonhoeffer to lay their lives on the line. And Navarre, who kept his kingdom, brought Christian tolerance to France for almost a century.

The Teshuvah journey to unity in Christ is based on our love of God.

Jesus replied, "Anyone who loves me will obey my teaching. My Father will love them, and we will come to them and make our home with them."

—JOHN 14:23

Choose to serve God so you can love Him and live in His presence.

℘ ℨ

The Teshuvah journey of Christ shows us how to respond to the Teshuvah invitation by choosing faith, obedience, and serving God. We can reverse the curse and live in God's presence, moving into our destiny.

For it is by grace you have been saved, through faith—and this not from yourselves, it is the gift of God—not by works, so that no one can boast. For we are God's handiwork, created in Christ Jesus to do good works, which God prepared in advance for us to do.

—EPHESIANS 2:8–10

CHAPTER 11

HEALING THE BROKEN BODY OF CHRIST

W E GIVE GREAT credit to Pope Francis, whose 2014 video to a Kenneth Copeland pastor's conference, greeting them as brothers in Christ and inviting them to come together with him, began the unity revival.

But it was Jesus Himself who initiated the unity movement with His prayer for unity the night before He was crucified.

> *My prayer is not for them alone. I pray also for those who will believe in me through their message, that all of them may be one, Father, just as you are in me and I am in you. May they also be in us so that the world may believe that you have sent me. I have given them the glory that you gave me, that they may be one as we are one—I in them and you in me—so that they may be brought to complete unity. Then the world will know that you sent me and have loved them even as you have loved me.*
>
> —JOHN 17:20–23

To Jesus, the key to unity came when the believers were in Christ, united with Him in the same way He was united with the Father. This is the same unity pictured in the Teshuvah solar eclipse where the moon, symbolizing the believers, is in the sun, symbolizing Christ. Thus, the first step toward Christian unity is for individual believers to make the Teshuvah journey to return to God and come into unity in Christ. Those who refuse to be in Christ—the Muslims, Hindus, atheists, and other non-believers—cannot enter into unity with Christians. Only those united in Christ can achieve true Christian unity.

Almost since the beginning of Christianity, believers have quarreled about Christian doctrine and church government. The first Jerusalem Council served as an example of a favorably resolved dispute (Acts 15). However, other disputes resulted in division and treatment of opponents as non-Christians. For example, some Protestants who believe in salvation only through faith will recite many doctrinal differences with Catholics, claiming those make them un-Christian although Catholics share their belief in salvation only through faith. The critics have forgotten the words of the apostle Paul, "Accept one another, then, just as Christ accepted you" (Rom. 15:7).

Instead of myriad doctrinal tests, the apostle Paul tells how to know if we are in Christ:

> If you declare with your mouth, "Jesus is Lord," and believe in your heart that God raised him from the dead, you will be saved. For it is with your heart that you believe and are justified, and it is with your mouth that you profess your faith and are saved.
> —ROMANS 10:9–10

In other words, those who are justified by faith and say so are in Christ. If you are in Christ and those with whom you disagree are in Christ, you are united with them in Christ whether you admit it or not.

Although our unity comes through Christ, many denominations and doctrines create a great diversity within the body of Christ. Lutheran theologian Oscar Cullmann said, "Unity in the church...is unity in diversity...recognizing others in all their variety as true Christians."[1] Pope Francis has said, "Unity brought by the Spirit can harmonize every diversity."[2] Unity in diversity recognizes the contributions of other streams of Christianity and blends them together in a symphony of harmony. It is a unity of the Spirit, not in doctrine or church government.

The church has come a long way since the sixteenth and seventeenth centuries, when being a Protestant in France or a Catholic in England could be a death sentence. The French Edict of Nantes, in effect for less than a century, and the English Act of Tolerance were important steps toward Paul's admonition to accept brother Christians. The revivalists of the Great Awakening and the second Great Awakening first transcended their denominations, achieving a forerunner of unity in diversity. The Charismatic movement brought about spiritual unity, as Christians across many denominations shared in the same experiences and often worshiped together.

The Catholic Church has led the way in bringing about spiritual unity. It began when Leo XIII started the Catholic Church praying every year for a new Pentecost and Christian unity. During the Second Vatican Council, Pope John XXIII initiated the acceptance of the genuine Christianity practiced by other denominations and opened the door to the Holy Spirit. Then, as the Charismatic Renewal caught fire, the Catholic Church embraced it and the spiritual unity it brought. And, along with the Lutherans, the Catholic Church accepted the doctrine of salvation by faith, effectively ending the division that started the Protestant Reformation.

The high point of charismatic spiritual unity came in 1977, when fifty thousand Catholics and charismatic Christians from many denominations gathered in Kansas City to worship together and move in unity. A highlight of the meeting was recognition that the body of Christ was broken and prayer for its healing. Yet, after 1977, the denominational charismatics began drifting apart, not in anger or disunity but in complacency. They still loved one another and conducted occasional joint meetings, but accomplishments were minimal.

The International Star Bible Society believes we have come to an appointed time, a sacred season, to pick up where the 1977 Kansas City meeting left off. We believe the blood moon tetrad of 2014–2015, the ninth since Christ, was a heavenly sign of a great unity revival, as the blood moon tetrad of 1967–1968 was a heavenly sign of the Charismatic revival.[3] The Teshuvah eclipse of 2017, which passes over Kansas City, is a heavenly sign of the church's call to return to God and its unity in Christ. God wants to heal the broken body of Christ.

The Unity Revival has already begun. The pope's outreach to Kenneth Copeland in 2014 produced a flood of Christian leaders who traveled to Rome for international reconciliation meetings. There have also been national-level events like Azusa Now: The Call in Los Angeles, where Lou Engle and Matteo Calisi led historic prayers for reconciliation between Christians. Much has happened, but much more needs to happen to heal the broken body of Christ.

The urgent need to heal the body of Christ must be communicated from the national leadership of movements and denominations to the local churches. The city fathers must become champions of unity, bringing the body of Christ together to impact their communities. The prayer of Jesus in John 17 is not only about unity. It is for unity with a purpose, "So that the world may believe" (John 17:21).

Like the watchmen on the wall in the Teshuvah scripture of Ezekiel 33, the church must warn the unbelievers of the judgment to come and bring as many as possible to salvation. The body of Christ must be healed to do its work for Christ.

Chapter 12
HEALING THE LAND

THE TESHUVAH ECLIPSE passing over the United States on August 21, 2017, is an invitation for believers and the church to come back to God and be united in Christ. It is also a solemn warning that we ignore at our peril.

The warning is made all the more urgent because, when the sky goes dark in the total eclipse, the bright star Regulus will be seen only two degrees from the eclipse. Regulus, meaning "treading under foot," is the brightest star in the constellation Leo, the lion, which pictures the judgment and destruction of Christ's enemies. The nearness of the eclipse to Regulus, one of the brightest stars in the night sky, warns us that judgment is near.

Many Christians hope the results of the 2016 election will save America. The truth is, America is in deep spiritual trouble, and the outcome of the election will only delay the country's slide downward into degeneration. Without a Teshuvah repentance and return to God, America may follow the path of Germany into destruction.

The study of Germany's Teshuvah choices shows that it was the home of the Protestant reformation and once was a shining light for God, just like America. But Germany began to lose its way as its academic institutions used flimsy theories to destroy the faith of many, similar to what American universities do now. In the late nineteenth century the German government successfully diminished the role of the church in public life and substituted for it the state, while in America this process began in the 1960s. Then, once the German Christians had been desensitized to the Scriptures and God's voice, the curse of Satan's throne came to Berlin. The curse in America is the abomination of abortion.

In the 1880s, judgments began to fall on Germany, but slowly at first. The kaiser's son, who would have been an able ruler, died shortly after the death of the kaiser, leaving the country in the hands of an unqualified individual who misruled the nation. From 2009 to January 2017, the United States endured questionable leadership, leading to economic decline, international decline, political decline, and moral decline. Germany went on to become entangled in balance-of-power politics, a trap that is being set for us, and bumbled into the disastrous World War I. Failing to learn its lesson, Germany elected an anti-Christian demagogue, Adolf Hitler, who initiated the Holocaust and led the country to destruction in World War II, as most Christians stood by and let it happen. All of these things can happen in America. After all, Hitler killed 6 million Jews, but our courts and politicians have allowed abortionists to kill 58 million babies, almost ten times as many as the Holocaust, by 2016.

The blame for the German tragedy sits squarely on the shoulders of the church. Instead of exposing the fallacy of the faith-killing theories about the Bible, the church taught them in its seminaries. The state takeover of the church's place in the public square was applauded as progress. Having lost its scriptural foundation, the church did not understand the curse arising from the throne of Satan. The church failed to pray for healing of the good ruler and meekly accepted the misrule of his son. No objection was raised to the increasing militarization of the country, and when World War I came, the church dutifully supported it. Hitler was a known anti-democracy fascist but came into office to restore order. Then, as his crimes mounted up and he started World War II, the church as a whole kept silent. To put it in the context of Jesus's Teshuvah teaching, they lost their faith, they tested God, and they sold out to His enemies.

The amazing thing about the judgments that befell Germany, including its dismemberment by the victorious Russians for over forty years, is that God is still trying to use the German church. It was their prayers that brought down the Berlin Wall in 1989 and brought a new hope of freedom to Eastern Europe. God never gives up.

God also has been especially merciful to America. He kept the Jamestown Colony from total destruction and saved the Puritans from massacre in Massachusetts when they repented after backsliding. He sent the first and second Great Awakenings to revive a people who were not following Him. He held the nation together in its revolution, the formation of its government, and the Civil War over slavery. He sent the Azusa Street Revival, revival through Billy Graham and the tent revivalists, and the Charismatic movement. And now, even though the nation has been under judgment since 2001, He is sending the Unity Revival, signified by the blood moon tetrad of 2014–2015. God is not through with America yet.

Second Chronicles 7:14 makes it clear that God's answer to healing our land is the church:

> *If my people, who are called by my name, will humble themselves and pray and seek my face and turn from their wicked ways, then I will hear from heaven, and I will forgive their sin and will heal their land.*

"IF MY PEOPLE, WHO ARE CALLED BY MY NAME"

There is no other way to bring heaven's answers to Earth than through the church.

"WILL HUMBLE THEMSELVES"

We cannot blame our problems on the Republicans or the Democrats, the government or the media, or even the voters who elect corrupt politicians. The church cannot stand proudly above the storm, full of judgment and condemnation, and deny responsibility. No, we must humble ourselves and admit that it is our failure to portray the love of God in our generation that has brought us to this place.

"AND PRAY"

We must understand that God has the answers, and we do not. We must hear from heaven and walk out God's strategies. As Jesus taught us to pray, "Your will be done, on earth as it is in heaven" (Matt. 6:10), our job is not so much to force change as it is to release the power of God through prayer and cooperate in bringing about God's solution.

"AND SEEK MY FACE"

King David tells us to give thanks, sing, and praise God, testifying about Him and rejoicing as we seek His face (1 Chron. 16:8–11). The Teshuvah psalm, Psalm 27, is a prayer to live in the presence of God and seek His face. Jesus said that those who obey His command to love their brothers are friends of God, knowing His business (John 15:15). God wants us to seek His face and know Him so well that we are His friends, loving and united with our fellow Christians. We will then be partners in bringing His plans to pass.

"AND TURN FROM THEIR WICKED WAYS"

The church must make the Teshuvah journey of repentance and return to God. We must act with Christian love if the land is to be healed.

- *Come into visible unity* so the world will have faith in Christ. The divisions in the church are a scandal and a slander on Christ. Many souls have been lost because of our divisions, and many will be saved if we unify.

- *Bless and curse not.* It is blessings that bring change,[1] like turning on a light instead of cursing the darkness. By blessing and loving our enemies, we are partnering with God in His plan to save them and fulfilling God's call that we be a blessing (1 Pet. 3:9).

- *Transcend politics.* Christians in both political parties must overcome political agendas that divide them. Christians should not retreat from the public square but instead should see that Christian principles are reflected in the policies of both political parties.

- *Awake from a slumbering spirit.* The church still claims a majority of Americans, yet most Christians are slumbering, happy to be complacent. The church needs to wake up and influence society before it is too late.

To save the nation we must individually make our Teshuvah journey, like Jesus did, coming to unity with God. The church must also make its Teshuvah journey of repentance and uniting in Christ.

Then, as we seek God's face, we will pray for a great revival in America that will take the nation on a Teshuvah journey of repentance back into unity with God and return it to its calling as a Christian nation and a light to the world.

God is sending His sign, the Teshuvah eclipse of 2017, as His invitation and His warning. We must choose life or death, blessings or curses.

Choose life before it is too late.

Chapter 13

THE TESHUVAH 2017 PILGRIMAGE

To make the Teshuvah journey into God's presence during the times of ancient Israel meant making a pilgrimage to the temple in Jerusalem.

> *Blessed are those whose strength is in you, whose hearts are set on pilgrimage. As they pass through the Valley of Baka, they make it a place of springs; the autumn rains also cover it with pools. They go from strength to strength, till each appears before God in Zion.*
>
> —Psalm 84:5–7

Psalm 84 tells us that God blesses those who make a pilgrimage to His presence. They are refreshed by streams and pools, symbolic of the Holy Spirit, and grow stronger as they approach God. Even in the church age, when the Holy Spirit lives within us, the spiritual value of the pilgrimage as a symbolic return to God has been recognized and honored. On August 21, 2017, we can make such a pilgrimage by traveling to a location along the Teshuvah eclipse path as a sign of our commitment to return to God.

The path of the eclipse will run from Oregon through fourteen states, ending in South Carolina.[1] Anyone wanting to make the pilgrimage will need to seek the face of the Lord for guidance in choosing a location.[2] We will also have the opportunity to bless the site of our pilgrimage by adding our prayers for that place to our prayers for personal repentance and return to God, for the healing of the broken body of Christ, and for healing of our land.

The eclipse will make landfall at Lincoln Beach in Oregon at 10:15 am PST. Unlike the sun, which travels from east to west, the eclipse shadow travels from west to east and symbolizes the turning back of repentance. About an hour and a half later, the shadow will leave the United States at Cape Romaine, South Carolina. The shadow will remain over locations near the center of the path of totality for about two minutes.

Information about the eclipse path and some local prayer needs[3] are shown below.

OREGON

The eclipse passes over Salem, the capital, at 10:17 am PST. The state of Oregon has a relatively low number of Christians, between 60 and 75 percent but has been identified as a key state to bring God's people to stand in unity against secularism and what stands against God. It was in Oregon that a Christian baker was fined for refusing to participate in a homosexual wedding and schools began permitting alleged transgender boys to invade girls' restrooms and even shower with them. Religious freedom and Christian values are under strong attack in Oregon. Pray the state will be blessed with an outpouring of the Holy Spirit and Christian love.

The church in Oregon has been praying for numbers of prophetic Christians to come join them in prayer, and the Teshuvah pilgrimage presents an opportunity for this to happen.

IDAHO

The eclipse arrives in Idaho at 11:33 am MST, but there are no major cities in its path. Idaho also has a relatively low Christian population, 60 to 75 percent, and the largest religious group is the Mormon Church. We should pray the Mormon Church will be blessed by a true revelation of Jesus. The state has many natural and spiritual treasures that should be called forth. Prayer leaders in Idaho have prayed for reconciliation, intimacy in worship, and joy.

Montana

The path of totality only covers eight square miles of Montana. Nevertheless, the state is important because it has a breaker anointing. Pray for the church to be blessed with a new impartation of this anointing.

The church in Montana has prayed for purity and Christian unity, as Jesus prayed in John 17.

Wyoming

The eclipse passes over Grand Teton National Park at 11:35 am MST and Casper at 11:42 am MST. The state has been a leader in bringing equal rights to women and has sought to maintain godly laws. The state is known as a place to retreat for renewal and peace. Pray the church will continue in faithfulness and be blessed by achieving its destiny.

Prayer leaders have prayed for unity and a habitation of God's Spirit.

Nebraska

The eclipse runs through the length of Nebraska, reaching the capital of Lincoln at 1:02 pm CST. The state plays a vital role in feeding America and the world. Pray the state will be blessed with pure and abundant waters above and below ground. Also pray the Joseph anointing will be released to bring provision and blessings to God's people and works.

The church in Nebraska has been admonished to tear down the false idol of humanism, come together in unity, and reverse the curse on the land.

Iowa

Only a small portion of southwest Iowa is touched by the eclipse. However, it has been prophesied that major political change in Iowa and beyond will begin in the southwest corner of the state. It is a forerunner for presidential politics and often highlights Christian issues.

Pray to bless the state with wisdom, clarity of purpose, and unity.

KANSAS

The eclipse reaches northeast Kansas at 1:06 pm CST. There is a well of revival in Kansas from the beginning of the modern Pentecostal outpouring in Kansas by Charles Parham that has been prophesied to be uncapped and bring hope and faith to many. Pray that there will be healing for those whose faith has been weakened by deferred hope for a move of God. Pray the church will be blessed and be a blessing to receive its inheritance.

MISSOURI

Missouri is the lynchpin of the Teshuvah eclipse path. Three major cities in the path of the eclipse have been identified as centers for the release of evangelism:

> Kansas City, Missouri, is passed over in its northern half at 1:06 pm CST. It is in Kansas City that the high point of the Charismatic Renewal unity movement was reached in 1977. Another great gathering is scheduled for October 2017 and will focus on unity in Christ and the evangelism coming from Christian unity, as Jesus prayed in John 17.[4]

> Jefferson City, the state capital, is reached at 1:14 pm CST. It has been prophesied that God does not need a majority to bring His plans to pass. Pray for wisdom and unity.

> St. Louis will be covered in its southern half at 1:16 pm CST. The city, still suffering from the Ferguson debacle, is in need of reconciliation

between races and churches and to see visible unity and the love of God expressed by Christians. Pray for an outpouring of love and forgiveness and for God to bring peace to the city.

ILLINOIS

Southern Illinois is passed over by the eclipse at 1:19 am CST. The state is undergoing a great shaking from violence in Chicago and poor financial policies in Springfield. Pray the legacy of liberty and forgiveness of the Great Emancipator, Abraham Lincoln, will be reborn in the state. Pray for restoration of racial harmony and unity.

Prayer leaders have seen a new connecting of the body of Christ and a new outpouring of grace, which will make a new net for the harvest.

KENTUCKY

The eclipse passes over southwestern Kentucky at 1:22 pm CST. Intercessors in Kentucky have focused on the Teshuvah scripture of Ezekiel 33 and accepted their role as watchmen on the wall to warn both the sinners and the righteous. They are praying for a new great awakening, remembering that the second Great Awakening began in Kentucky. Pray blessings for revelation and divine strategies to bring revival to America.

TENNESSEE

The eclipse reaches Nashville, the state capital and a national entertainment center, at 1:27 pm CST. The Lord has healed a historical curse of covenant-breaking because of the state's support for Israel, and the Lord has promised to bring the body of Christ together in a new level of unity. Pray that the musicians in Nashville will be blessed with a new love for Christ and a deeper desire for worship. Pray that the blessings of unity will be made real for those who, even now, are opposed to unity.

NORTH CAROLINA

At 2:34 pm EST, the eclipse reaches southwestern North Carolina and the Great Smoky Mountains National Park. The state has taken a stand for godly values, and the Lord is using the state in the battle to cleanse and heal our land. Pray that the state will be blessed for the persecution it is enduring and pray that the eyes of the persecutors will be opened. The Lord has promised to change the heavens over the state to bring in a new direction for revival.

GEORGIA

Northwest Georgia sees the eclipse at 2:35 pm EST. The state, once home to racial division and violence, has made great strides in achieving racial reconciliation. Pray that God will bless Georgia with a spirit of love and brotherhood between races, ethnic groups, and Christian denominations.

The Lord has promised an open portal under heaven for revelation, worship, and restoration, along with reversal of the curse of racial hostility and violence.

SOUTH CAROLINA

The eclipse reaches Columbia, the state capital, at 2:41 pm EST, Charleston at 2:48 pm EST, and leaves the United States at 2:49 pm EST. In 2003 the prophets warned South Carolina that God was giving them another chance to break the stronghold of division, racism, and secularism that had plagued the state. Twelve years later, after a horrible mass murder by a white man in a Charleston black church, the nation was amazed to see a spirit of reconciliation and forgiveness drive out the attempts to bring racial strife into the city. Even some journalists understood the peace of Charleston was the result of Christians acting in love and unity.[5]

The other part of the 2003 word promised that there would be a disconnect from past cycles of failure through repentance and forgiveness. So, the state that started the American Civil War took down its defiant Confederate state flag, its symbol of rebellion and racism, and broke the curse on the state.

Pray for continued blessings and healing of divisions in South Carolina.

ॐ ॐ

The first landfall of the Teshuvah eclipse in Oregon shows us there is much work to do to reverse the curse, heal the broken body of Christ, and heal our land. But the last stop of the eclipse in South Carolina shows us that God can bring His people together to heal their land.

This is the Teshuvah hope we have, as explained by Dutch Sheets in his 2003 prophecy to South Carolina:

> God doesn't just ignore our history—He heals history.[6]

Chapter 14
PRAYING THROUGH TESHUVAH

THE FIRST DAY of Teshuvah 2017 will feature the spectacular United States total eclipse. We hope many make the pilgrimage to experience the eclipse in person or at least view it on media outlets that will carry the event. Even more, we hope many will take the forty-day Teshuvah journey to return to God, pray for God's people, and pray for healing of our land.

Teshuvah presents all of us with the choice of life or death, blessings or curses, as described in Deuteronomy 31:19–20. The position of the Teshuvah eclipse in the heavens shows the same choice.[1] During the eclipse, the stars will become visible, with the stars of the constellation Leo to the east of the eclipse and those of Cancer to the west. The constellation Cancer, meaning "the holding place," represents the home of God's people, which is commonly known as heaven. The constellation Leo, representing Christ as the Lion of Judah, pictures God's judgment, which we commonly describe as hell. Thus, the Teshuvah eclipse illustrates the choice between life and heaven on one hand, and death and hell on the other.

During the days from the August 21 eclipse date to August 31, we invite you to join with us in the International Star Bible Society in praying through this devotional schedule for personal repentance, reversing the curse, and choosing life.

- ✦ August 21: Choose life (Deut. 31:19–20)

- ✦ August 22: The victorious forty-day Teshuvah journey of Jesus (Matt. 4:1–11; John 14:32)

- ✦ August 23: We are children of God (Rom. 8:12–15)

- August 24: Faith (Deut. 8:1–5)

- August 25: No condemnation for those in
  Christ (Rom. 8:1–2)

- August 26: Obedience (Deut. 6:17–26)

- August 27: Forgiveness (John 1:19)

- August 28: Love God (Deut. 6:4–15)

- August 29: Love brings obedience and peace
  (John 14:23)

- August 30: Tonight in the early evening look up
  to the zenith and find the star Vega, meaning
  "He shall be exalted," in the constellation Lyra,
  the harp, which pictures a dove and a harp and
  speaks of the role of worship in exalting Christ.
  Our solar system is moving toward Vega at
  forty thousand miles per hour, illustrating
  that we are destined for worship, so enter into
  His presence with worship and celebrate your
  destination.

- August 31: Make sure you have received
  salvation by grace to achieve your destiny (Gal.
  2:8–10)

Associated with the heavenly constellation of Cancer are
two constellations which represent God's people. In the
northwestern sky after sunset is the constellation we call the
Big Dipper, which the Israelites called the Assembly. This is
the same name as the Greek word for the church, and the
meaning is confirmed by its stars, Alkaid, "the assembly," and
Dubeh Lachar, "the latter herd." At the top of the sky the
other constellation, known popularly as the Little Dipper,

is really "the lesser sheepfold." It represents those believers before Christ came, who are named by the star Kochab, "waiting on Him who comes." God's plan to unify the believers is shown in the constellation Pisces, the fish: a picture of two fish, representing the Jews and the Gentiles, which are joined together by the unifying constellation the Band.

From September 1 to September 10, we will be praying for God's people and the healing of the broken body of Christ as God's people come together united in Christ.

+ September 1: The blessings of unity (Ps. 133)

+ September 2: Unity in Christ (John 17:20–22)

+ September 3: Accepting our brothers (Rom. 15:5–7)

+ September 4: Do not judge (Rom. 14:13; Luke 6:37–38)

+ September 5: Divisions (1 Cor. 3:1–9)

+ September 6: Evangelism through unity (John 17:23)

+ September 7: Watchmen warnings (Ezek. 33)

+ September 8: Appealing to all (1 Cor. 9:27)

+ September 9: Salvation for Israel (Rom. 11:11–32)

+ September 10: Messianic Jews and the Toward Jerusalem Council II (Acts 15)

In the early evening of September 11, the sixteenth anniversary of the 9/11 attacks on America, the stars will present a vivid picture of God's dealings with the rebelliousness of men and nations. In the southwestern sky stands the constellation Scorpio, the scorpion, which is a picture of rebellious men. (See Ezekiel 2:6; Luke 10:18.) Standing just above Scorpio is the constellation Ophiuchus, the serpent-holder: a picture of a giant man, representing Christ, who is restraining a serpent, representing Satan, and who is poised to crush the rebellious scorpion underfoot. Finally, above Ophiuchus is the constellation Hercules, the mighty victor, showing a man, Christ, who is punishing a three-headed serpent, which represents the rebellious nations. The heavens show us that the Lord will restrain evil but will also punish rebellious men and nations.

Beginning with September 11 and continuing through September 19, we will pray for the restraint of evil and the healing of our land.

+ September 11: We repent for the nation (Isaiah 9:8–10; scriptures about defiance against God, spoken rebelliously by United States leaders as they refused to repent after the 9/11 attack)

+ September 12: Blessings and curses (Deut. 28)

+ September 13: Healing the land (2 Cor. 7:14)

+ September 14: Humility (Matt. 23:12)

+ September 15: Bringing heaven to Earth (Matt. 6:16)

+ September 16: Praying in confidence (1 John 5:14–15)

+ September 17: Protection in God's presence (Ps.27)

+ September 18: Bless and curse not (1 Peter 3:9)

+ September 19: Friends of God (John 15:4)

The last ten days of Teshuvah cover the period from the Feast of Trumpets, known more popularly as Rosh Hashanah, "the head of the tear," through the Day of Atonement. This period is considered by the Jews to be a time of heightened importance and is called Days of Awe. The prophetic understanding of these feasts is truly awesome, as the Feast of Trumpets is believed to represent the second coming of Christ, and the Day of Atonement represents God's judgment.

+ September 20: Trumpets: The Second Coming (Matt. 24:29–31)

+ September 21: Resurrection of the believers (1 Cor. 15:50–58; Rev. 20:4–6)

+ September 22: On this date the sun leaves the judgment constellation of Leo and moves into the constellation Virgo, the virgin, which is the first book of the Star Bible and pictures the promise of Genesis 3:15 to bring the Seed of Woman, Christ, who will be bruised in the heel, the Cross, and crush the head of the serpent, Satan. In the western sky stands the constellation Bootes, "the coming one," associated with Virgo, which pictures one "like the Son of Man," Christ, who will harvest the Earth when He returns (Rev. 14:14–16). This is one of the many signs in the sun, moon, and stars that say Jesus is coming back.

+ September 23: Come, Lord Jesus (Rev. 22:12–17)

+ September 24: Be ready (Matt. 24:36–51)

+ September 25: Rising in the northeast in the early evening is the constellation Perseus, the breaker, which represents the triumph of Christ over the men and nations opposing Him when He returns. The judgment of the head of the nations, the Antichrist, is shown by the star Algol, "evil spirit," which is pictured as a severed head held by Perseus (Rev. 16:13–14).

+ September 26: Judging our works (1 Cor. 3:11–15)

+ September 27: The sheep and goats (Matt. 25:31–46)

+ September 28: The great white throne judgment (Rev. 20:11–15)

On Friday, September 29, the Teshuvah season ends with the Day of Atonement, also called Yom Kippur. We have prayed earnestly for the healing of the broken body of Christ and the healing of our nation at this *kairos* appointed time. In the end the church and the nation must choose life or death, blessings or curses, and we will have to wait and see what the outcome may be.

You, on the other hand, can control your own level of spiritual power by making the Teshuvah journey back to God and uniting in Christ. When Jesus sent out seventy-two believers into a dark land of stubborn, sinful people to preach and heal, they were amazed at the power they had. Their evangelistic ministry produced the only biblical record of a dark principality, Satan, falling out of the heavenly places (Luke 10:1–20).

As you reach the end of your Teshuvah journey and take stock on the Day of Atonement, remember the heavenly image of Jesus restraining the snake and preparing to crush the scorpion in the constellation Ophiuchus. Be encouraged by the words that Jesus spoke to His seventy-two evangelists:

> *I have given you authority to trample on snakes and scorpions and to overcome all the power of the enemy; nothing will harm you. However, do not rejoice that the spirits submit to you, but rejoice that your names are written in heaven.*
>
> —LUKE 10:19–20

TABLE OF TESHUVAH ECLIPSES

TESHUVAH ECLIPSE YEAR	PASSOVER AND TABERNACLES BLOOD MOONS	LOCAL MESSAGES
1495, 1496	1493, 1494	Caribbean
1505	-	-
1514	1512	-
1523, 1524	1522	-
1533	-	-
1542, 1543	1541	China
1560, 1561	1559	-
1571	-	-
1589	-	-
1598	1595	-
1607, 1608	1606	Virginia
1627, 1628	1624	-
1644, 1645	1642	-
1654, 1655	1653	England
1672, 1673, 1674	1671	New England
1691, 1692	1689	-
1701	-	-
1710	1707	-

1495–2018

Party	Event or Message
Spanish	End forced conversion
Indians	Repent and be saved
Martin Luther	Serve God
Martin Luther	Saved by faith
Lutherans	Lawlessness
Henry VIII	English Reformation
Francis Xavier	Asian evangelism
Elizabeth I	Anglican Church
Catholic Church	Council of Trent
Charles IX	St. Bartholomew's Day Massacre
Phillip II	War on England
Henry of Navarre	Edict of Nantes
Jamestown	Seek God's plan
Samuel de Champlain	Indian missions
Pilgrims	Wait on God
Pilgrims	Migration to America
Germans	Thirty Years' War
Puritans	Civil war
Oliver Cromwell	Do not force revival
Puritans	Complacency
William of Orange	Act of Toleration
English	War of Spanish Succession
English	National unity

TABLE OF TESHUVAH ECLIPSES

TESHUVAH ECLIPSE YEAR	PASSOVER AND TABERNACLES BLOOD MOONS	LOCAL MESSAGES
1719, 1720	-	-
1737, 1738, 1739	1736	-
1756, 1757	1754	Quebec
1766	-	-
1775	1772	-
1784, 1785	1783	-
1802, 1803, 1804	1801	-
1821, 1822	1819	Mexico
1831	-	-
1840	-	Central Africa
1849, 1850	1848	-
1867, 1868,1869	1866	-
1886, 1887	1884	Germany
1896	1894	-
1905	1902	-
1914, 1915	1913	Russia
	-	-

1495–2018 (continued)

PARTY	EVENT OR MESSAGE
Count Nicolaus Zinzendorf	Revival prayer
George Whitfield	Great Awakening
French	Loss from intolerance
Thirteen colonies	Conflict with England
Thirteen colonies	American Revolution
George Washington	American unity
William Carey	Foreign missions
French	French Revolution
Barton Stone	Second Great Awakening
Mexicans	Mexican Revolution
English	Opening China
Dr. Livingstone	Opening Africa
Americans	Civil War
Hudson Taylor	China Inland Missions
Kaiser Wilhelm I	Losing faith
Pope Leo XIII	Prayer for Pentecost
Theodor Herzl	Zionism
Charles Parham	Outpouring of Holy Spirit
William Seymour	Azuza St. Revival
Czar Nicholas	Communism
Chiam Weitzmann	Balfour Declaration

TABLE OF TESHUVAH ECLIPSES

Teshuvah Eclipse Year	Passover and Tabernacles Blood Moons	Local Messages
1932, 1933, 1934	1931	Israel
1952	1949, 1950	-
1961	-	-
1970	1967, 1968	-
1979, 1980	1978	-
1998, 1999	1996	Afghanistan Germany
2008	-	China, Russia
2017, 2018	2014, 2015	United States

1495–2018 *(continued)*

Party	Event or Message
David Ben-Gurion	Holocaust
German Church	Nazi apocalypse
Billy Graham	American Revival
Pope John XXIII	Second Vatican Council
American Church	Attack through courts
American Church	Charismatic revival
Marty Chernoff	Messianic Judaism
Israelis	Complacency after 1967 Six Days' War
Ronald Regan	Overthrow of communism
Jimmy Carter	Rise of militant Islam
Israelis	Peace with Egypt
American Church	Warning of 9/11 attack
Lutherans and Catholics	End of protest
Americans	Decline of the United States
Israelis	Mideast wars
American Church	Unite to heal our land

NOTES

PREFACE

1. Our book, The Mystery of the Blood Moons (Lake Mary, FL: Creation House, 2015), examines the blood moons from a scriptural and historic viewpoint.

2. We recommend welder's glass for direct viewing of the sun. Do not look directly at the sun, and do not point binoculars or a telescope toward the sun. You may safely look at an eclipse only during the short period of totality when the sun is completely darkened.

3. George Santayana, The Life of Reason (1905), quoted at "Those who fail to learn from history..." National Churchill Museum, November 16, 2012, available at https://www. nationalchurchillmuseum.org/blog/churchill-quote-history/ (accessed April 20, 2017).

CHAPTER 1:
DISCOVERING TESHUVAH ECLIPSES

1. The prophetic message was given by Chuck Pierce at the End-Time Handmaidens and Servants 23rd Annual Convention in Dallas, Texas, on July 8, 1998.

2. The dates and pathways of solar eclipses are taken from the classic work of Prof. Theodore Von Oppolzer, Canon of Eclipses (New York, NY: Dover Publications, Inc., 1992).

3. There was a Teshuvah eclipse in 2008, which will be discussed in chapter 7.

CHAPTER 2:
THE SIGN OF THE TESHUVAH ECLIPSES

1. The revelation of Christ in the heavens is described in our book, International Star Bible Society, The Stars of His Coming (Dallas, TX: Praise River Production Corp, 2012).

2. The meaning and history associated with the blood moon tetrads on Passover and Tabernacles are covered in our book The Mystery of the Blood Moons.

CHAPTER 3:
THE BROKEN BODY OF CHRIST

1. The prayer and other excerpts from the 1977 Kansas City meeting can be seen on the United in Christ website, www.unitedinchrist.net.

2. The agreement is contained in the Joint Declaration on the Doctrine of Justification by the Lutheran World Federation and the Catholic Church, dated October 31, 1999. It can be found on the United in Christ website, www.unitedinchrist.net.

CHAPTER 4:
TOLERATION

1. We highly recommend the trilogy of books by Peter Marshall and David Manuel, *The Light and the Glory* (Grand Rapids, MI: Fleming H. Revell, 1977), *From Sea to Shining Sea* (Grand Rapids, MI: Fleming H. Revell, 1977), and *Sounding Forth the Trumpet* (Grand Rapids, MI: Fleming H. Revell, 1998) to anyone interested in the Christian roots and history of the United States.

CHAPTER 5:
UNITY IN DIVERSITY

1. The quotation is take from Joseph Ratzinger, *The Ratzinger Reader: Mapping a Theological Journey*, Lieven Boeve and Gerard Mannion, eds. (New York: Bloomsbury T&T Clark, 2010), 170. More information on the concept of unity in diversity can be found in the *Unity in Reconciled Diversity* pamphlet of United in Christ and other publications available on the www.unitedinchrist.net website.

2. *Annals of America, Vol II* (Chicago, IL: Encyclopedia Britannica, 1968), 276, quoted in Marshall and Manuel, *The Light and the Glory*, 306.

3. We are indebted to Dutch Sheets, who in his book *An Appeal to Heaven* (Dallas, TX: Dutch Sheets Ministries, 2015), shows us the history of this flag and its significance for revival today.

CHAPTER 6:
CHRIST TO THE NATIONS

1. The story of the development of the Babylon religion, its spread across the Earth, its sister false religions, and its ultimate destruction is told in Corporate Prayer Resources, *Babylon: A Spiritual Journey Through Time and the Nations* (Dallas, TX: Praise River Production Corp., 2012), which is available as an e-book at www.corporateprayerresources.com.

2. For more information about the importance of the blood moon tetrad of 1493–1494 see our book *The Mystery of the Blood Moons.*

CHAPTER 7:
CALLING THE NATIONS TO REPENTANCE

1. Abraham Lincoln, "Proclamation 97—Appointing a Day of National Humiliation, Fasting, and Prayer," March 30, 1863, available at http://www.presidency.ucsb.edu/ws/?pid=69891 (accessed April 18, 2017).

2. There were 641,000 slaves counted in the 1790 United States Census (Marshall and Manuel, *Sea to Shining Sea*, 232).

3. This famous quotation is reproduced from George Grant and Wilbur Gregory, *The Christian Almanac* (Nashville, TN: Cumberland House, 2000), 138.

4. We recommended that you read Roger Lowenstein's excellent book, *The End of Wall Street* (New York: Penguin Books, 2011) to understand the 2008 financial collapse.

CHAPTER 8:
CALLED TO JERUSALEM

1. The revelation that President Obama had determined to withdraw from the Middle East was revealed in an interview in *The New York Times Magazine* given by Ben Rhodes, deputy national security advisor for strategic communications. The article, written by David Samuels, is titled "The Aspiring Novelist Who became Obama's Foreign Policy Guru," May 5, 2016, available at https://www.nytimes.com/2016/05/08/magazine/the-aspiring-

novelist-who-became-obamas-foreign-policy-guru.html?_r=0 (accessed April 18, 2017).

CHAPTER 9:
CALLED TO UNITY IN CHRIST

1. Quoted in Stanley M. Burgess and Eduard M. van der Maas, *The New International Dictionary of Pentecostal and Charismatic Movements: Revised and Expanded Edition* (Grand Rapids, MI: Zondervan, 2010), 36.

2. The quotation is from an advertisement for the Azusa Now meeting in the March 2016 issue of *Charisma* magazine, p. 31.

3. Matteo Calisi, a Catholic charismatic from Bari, Italy, began his reconciliation ministry after receiving a prophetic word from David du Plessis that he would be an ambassador of reconciliation. He has brought the message of unity to three popes and numerous Catholic, Protestant, Orthodox, and messianic leaders around the world. He is currently president of United in Christ, a ministry which seeks to bring reconciliation between Christians. The organization's website is www.unitedinchrist.net.

4. This quotation is from a paper written by Catholic charismatic leader Matteo Calisi, "The Future of the Catholic Charismatic Renewal," contained on page 69 of Vinson Synan, ed., *Spirit-Empowered Christianity in the 21st Century* (Lake Mary, FL: Charisma House, 2011).

5. The prophecy and prayer for unity is quoted in Dan Almeter, *Unity: On Earth as It Is in Heaven* (Augusta, GA: Alleluia Christian Service Center, Inc., 2014), 107. Dan is the leader of the Ecumenical Alleluia Community in Augusta, Georgia.

6. For more information about Toward Jerusalem Council II, see their website at www.TJCII.org.

7. For more information see our book *The Mystery of the Blood Moons.*

8. The video is available on the United in Christ website, www.unitedinchrist.net.

9. Details of this meeting are available at www.Kairos2017.com.

CHAPTER 11:
HEALING THE BROKEN BODY OF CHRIST

10. Oscar Cullman, *Unity Through Diversity* (1986), quoted in United in Christ, "United in Reconciled Diversity," http://unitedinchrist.com/documents/United-In-Christ-and-Unity-In-Reconciled-Diversity-news-release.pdf (accessed April 20, 2017).

11. Quoted from Pope Francis, *The Joy of the Gospel* (New York: Image, 2014).

12. For more detailed information see our book *The Mystery of the Blood Moons*.

CHAPTER 12:
HEALING THE LAND

1. This revelation is contained in a marvelous new book by Brad Burk called *Changing the Atmosphere* (North Charleston, SC: CreateSpace Independent Publishing Platform, 2016). For more information contact bradburk@juno.com.

CHAPTER 13:
THE TESHUVAH 2017 PILGRIMAGE

1. The path of the eclipse is available online at www.eclipse2017.org.

2. For more information see the website at www.Teshuvah2017.com.

3. Local prayer notes include portions of prophetic intercessory insights gathered by Chuck Pierce and Dutch Sheets during their 2003 and 2004 fifty-state tour, which is described in their book, *Releasing the Prophetic Destiny of a Nation* (Shippensburg, PA: Destiny Image Publishers, 2005).

4. For more information visit www.Kairos2017.com.

5. Daniel Henninger, a *Wall Street Journal* columnist, happened to be in Charleston at the time of the attack and gave his insights into the Christian response of Charleston in a *Wall Street Journal* column titled "What Charleston Knows," July 1,

2015, available at https://www.wsj.com/articles/what-charleston-knows-1435787143 (accessed April 18, 2017).

6.   Pierce and Sheets, *Releasing the Prophetic Destiny of a Nation*, 374.

CHAPTER 14:
PRAYER THROUGH TESHUVAH

1.   The information about the stars and constellations is drawn from our book *The Stars of His Coming*.

BIBLIOGRAPHY

Acemoglu, Daron and James Robinson, *Why Nations Fail* (New York, NY: Crown Publishers, 2012).

Aikman, David, *Jesus in Beijing* (Washington, DC: Regency Publishing Inc., 2003).

Allen, Ron, *The Mystery of the Blood Moons* (Lake Mary, FL: Creation House, 2015).

Almeter, Dan, *Unity on Earth as in Heaven* (Augusta, GA: Alleluia Christian Service Center, Inc., 2014).

Barker, Kenneth, ed., *The NIV Study Bible* (Grand Rapids, MI: Zondervan, 1985).

Bergreen, Laurence, *Columbus: The Four Voyages 1492–1504* (New York, NY: Penguin Group, 2012).

Blum, Howard, *Eve of Destruction* (New York NY: Harper Collins Publishers, 2003).

Burgess, Stanley M., and Gary B McGee, ed., *Dictionary of Pentecostal and Charismatic Movements* (Grand Rapids, MI: Regency Reference Library, 1988).

Burk, Brad, *Changing the Atmosphere* (Dallas, TX: Brad Burk, 2016).

Billy Graham Evangelistic Association, *Billy Graham, God's Ambassador* (Minneapolis, MN: Billy Graham Evangelistic Association, 1999).

Cahn, Jonathan, *The Harbinger* (Lake Mary, FL: Front Line, 2011).

Carr, Joseph, *The Twisted Cross* (Shreveport, LA: Huntingrton House Inc., 1985).

Corporate Prayer Resources, *Babylon: A Spiritual Journey Through Time and the Nations* (Dallas, TX: Praise River Production Corp., 2012).

Dallin, David G., and John F. Rothman, *Icon of Evil* (New York, NY: Random House, 2008).

Davidson, Marshall B., *The Horizon Concise History of France* (New York, NY: American Heritage Publishing Co., 1971).

Federer, William J., *America's God and Country* (Coppell, TX: FAME Publishing Inc., 1994).

Ferguson, Niall, *Empire* (New York, NY: Basic Books, 2003).

Finto, Don, *Your People Shall Be My People: How Israel and the Christian Church Will Come Together in the Last Days* (Ventura, CA: Gospel Light Publications, 2001).

Grant, George, and Wilbur Gregory, *The Christian Almanac* (Nashville, TN: Cumberland House, 2000).

Halley, Henry H., *Halley's Bible Handbook* (Grand Rapids, MI: Zondervan, 1965).

Herman, Arthur, *To Rule the Waves* (New York, NY: Harper Collins, 2014).

Hyatt, Eddie L., *2000 Years of Charismatic Christianity* (Tulsa, OK: Hyatt International Ministries, 1996).

International Star Bible Society, *The Stars of His Coming* (Dallas, TX: Praise River Production Corp, 2012).

Johnson, Todd M., and Kenneth R. Ross, eds., *Atlas of Global Christianity* (Edinburg, Scotland: Edinburg University Press, 2009).

Kitchener, Walther, *Russian History* (New York, NY: Harper Collins, 1991).

Levitt, Zola, *The Seven Feasts of Israel* (Dallas, TX: Zola Levitt, 1979).

Liardon, Roberts, *God's Generals* (Tulsa, OK: Albury Publishing, 1996).

Marshall, Peter, and David Manuel, *From Sea to Shining Sea* (Grand Rapids, MI: Fleming H. Revell, 1977).

Marshall, Peter, and David Manuel, *Sounding Forth the Trumpet* (Grand Rapids, MI: Fleming H. Revell, 1998).

Marshall, Peter, and David Manuel, *The Light and the Glory* (Grand Rapids, MI: Fleming H. Revell, 1977).

MacMillan, Margaret, *The War That Ended Peace* (New York, NY: Random House, 2013).

McDowell, Josh, *The New Evidence That Demands a Verdict* (Nashville, TN: Thomas Nelson Inc., 1999).

Meing, D. W., *The Shaping of America, Vol. I* (Binghamton, NY: Vail-Ballou Press, 1986).

Morgan, Kenneth O., ed., *The Oxford Illustrated History of Britain* (Oxford, England: Oxford University Pages, 1984).

Pierce, Chuck D., and Dutch Sheets, *Releasing the Prophetic Destiny of a Nation* (Shippensburg, PA: Destiny Image Publishers, Inc., 2005).

Reinhardt, Kurt F., *Germany: 2000 Years* (New York, NY: The Continuum Publishing Company, 1997).

Sheets, Dutch, *An Appeal to Heaven* (Dallas, TX: Dutch Sheets Ministries, 2015).

Shelly, Bruce L., *Christian History in Plain Language* (Dallas, TX: Word Publishing, 1982).

Synan, Vinson, Ed., *Spirit-Empowered Christianity in the 21st Century* (Lake Mary, FL: Charisma House, 2011).

Unger, Merrill F., *Unger's Bible Dictionary* (Chicago, IL: Moody Press, 1966).

Von Oppolzer, Prof. Theodore, *Canon of Eclipses* (New York, NY: Dover Publications, Inc., 1992).

ABOUT US

The International Star Bible Society is a Christian ministry dedicated to strengthening the faith of Christian believers by spreading God's message about Jesus Christ that is contained in the stars, which is known as the Star Bible.

Most modern Christians have shied away from the stars because of their association with pagan astrology or adopted an interest based on scientific findings. However, about one hundred and fifty years ago archeologists and linguists began to uncover the ancient names for the stars and constellations, names which told the same story found in the Bible. In these current times we know that God intended the stars for His children, and we are restoring the truth about the heavens.

We believe the understanding of how "the heavens declare the glory of God" is a moving testimony of the power and reality of God (Ps. 19:1). We have made this information available as an e-book, *The Stars of His Coming*, to tell this amazing story. It is also our hope to go beyond our present knowledge, which we feel has just scratched the surface of the revelation of the Star Bible.

Our second book, *The Mystery of the Blood Moons*, expands our knowledge of the Star Bible to show how God has blessed His people during the historical blood moon tetrads. It also gives us hope and direction for today.

This work expands on the understanding of the blood moon lunar eclipses by showing how the Teshuvah solar eclipses represent appointed times of God's invitation and warning. We pray that the Teshuvah eclipse of 2017 will mark a time of repentance and return God for individuals, the Cchurch, and the nation. For more information about the Teshuvah 2017 pilgrimage and prayer, see the website www.Teshuvah2017.com.

CONTACT US

We invite you to join us in this journey of faith.

International Star Bible Society

305 Spring Creek Village, Ste 518

Dallas, Texas 75248

Website: www.Starbiblesociety.com

E-mail: info@Starbiblesociety.com